Neil Simon Monologues

Dorl Meltzer

NEIL SIMON MONOLOGUES

Speeches from the Works of America's Foremost Playwright

Edited by Roger Karshner

delirium

I only fuck singers and journalists

ACTING EDITION

Dramaline® Publications

Dramaline Publications 36-851 Palm View Road
Rancho Mirage CA 92270
Phone 619/770-6076 fax 619/770-4507
Email: drama.line@gte.net
Web Site: dramaline.com

Library of Congress Cataloging-in-Publication-Data
Simon, Neil.
    Neil Simon Monologues: speeches from the works of America's foremost playwright / edited by Roger Karshner.
        p. cm.
    ISBN 0-940669-34-X
    1. Monologues. I. Karshner, Roger. II. Title
PS3537.I663A6 1996
812'.54—dc20   96-33841

Cover art by John Sabel

This book is printed on paper that meets the requirements of the American Standard of Permanence of paper for printed library material.

CONTENTS

FOREWORD

Most people are familiar with the fact that Neil Simon is the most successful playwright since Shakespeare. But most people are probably unaware of another noteworthy fact, namely that Neil Simon's words have probably been spoken more accurately by more actors than any playwright in modern history. There's a simple explanation for this. When an actor reads Neil's lines, he soon realizes that it is not just what has been written that makes the play so good. Each character has its own rhythm, and if you add or drop an "if, and, or but" from any of the lines, it just plain doesn't work. Though Neil is an avid rewriter, I have found that this fact remains constant in every version of any scene in any of his plays or films that I have been lucky enough to be involved in.

Neil also has one of the most acute senses of humor that I have ever known. Most people think that if a person has a sense of humor, it means that they appreciate and will respond to something funny. That is not what I mean. Responding to something humorous is an appreciation of humor. A sense of humor is an understanding of what will be funny if it is written with a certain dialogue or if a piece of "stage business" is executed in a certain way. Neil has as sharp of a true sense of humor as any writer I have ever known.

Most basic overall, I guess, is the God-given talent that Neil Simon possesses. He is a true, complete, and dedicated writer, and I just pray that he continues to be as generous as he has been in the past and continues to give us the same immense joy that he has for decades.

JACK LEMMON
BEVERY HILLS, CALIFORNIA
JANUARY, 1996

INTRODUCTION

This book offers the actor a wide range of speeches that are intended for workshop, audition and classroom use only. Attention should be given to the terms of copyright with specific attention to public performance.

Throughout the book, you will encounter "preceding" and "intervening" speeches that are presented in a different type-face. These speeches are not to be read and are included in the interest of orientation, duration and consistency.

The synopses of the plays cover major plot points and offer a general story outline. They will never, however, compensate for reading and studying the play scripts and viewing videos of the plays that have been brought to film (plays on video and laser are identified with a V or L or both under the title). All plays are published by Samuel French, Inc., with the exception of *The Star-Spangled Girl,* which is published by Dramatists Play Service

Editing these plays has been a rewarding experience because it has given me the opportunity of becoming intimate with their characters—funny, sad, tragic and endearing. I have been able to climb into their skin for a few moments and view the world from their perspective. It has been a rewarding journey. I trust that you will travel this same enriching road as you bring voice to Mr. Simon's people.

ROGER KARSHNER
RANCHO MIRAGE, CALIFORNIA
JANUARY, 1996

COME BLOW YOUR HORN

Premièred February 22, 1961
at the Brooks Atkinson Theatre, New York City

Directed by Stanley Prager

CAST

Alan Baker	Hal March
Peggy Evans	Arlene Golonka
Buddy Baker	Warren Berlinger
Mr. Baker	Lou Jacobi
Connie Dayton	Sarah Marshall
Mrs. Baker	Pert Kelton
A Visitor	Carolyn Brenner

The action of the play takes place in Alan's New York apartment.

Harry Baker is the proprietor of a waxed-fruit business and his two sons are in his employ: Alan, a profligate, malingerer and woman-izer; and Buddy, a dutiful, naive twenty-one-year-old who is still liv-ing at home. But Buddy is feeling the constraints of family ties and has decided to declare his independence. So he moves into Alan's bachelor apartment. Alan, more diligent in the pursuit of the good life than the waxed-fruit business, has jeopardized the Meltzer account. When his father demands that he regain the account "or else," Alan sets up a swinging party with Meltzer that backfires when their mother intervenes. Buddy's departure ruptures his relationship with his father, and Alan's blowing the Meltzer account results in his termination. So the two sons, or "bums" as their father calls them, are now on their own, disowned by their father.

Alan, distressed by being ostracized and unable to make an honest emotional commitment to his girlfriend, Connie, becomes more and more serious, but Buddy, thanks to lessons in "living" from the worldly Alan, becomes a self-confident swinger. This role reversal strains their relationship and leads to minor conflict. Then, Mother arrives with her suitcase, announcing that she can no longer tolerate her husband's intractability toward his sons. A final scene involving Alan, Buddy, Mother, Father, and Connie leads to understanding and resolution: Alan is marrying Connie and returning to the business, Mother and Father are off on a trip around the world. And Buddy? Buddy will be back marketing waxed fruit, too. He will also be living independently, pursuing the "good life."

Mother. ACT II.

Buddy, a naive and tentative young man, has finally mustered the nerve to leave home and has moved in with Alan, his profligate older brother. Alan, admonished by his father for blowing a deal with Martin Meltzer, an important business client, has abandoned a hot date and arranged a party at Meltzer's hotel as a means of assuaging him and saving the account. He has set up Buddy with the hot date, an aspiring actress, under the guise that Buddy is a Hollywood producer. Buddy, nervous, beside himself with apprehension, awaits her momentary arrival. The doorbell rings. He answers. Guess who? Mother! Buddy is now between a "hot date" and mother, a situation fraught with embarrassing possibilities. After a seemingly interminable period, Buddy has finally persuaded Mother to leave and has gone to the lobby to summon a taxi for her. In his absence, Buddy's mother takes a number of phone calls, which serve to tangle Alan's web.

MOTHER

Don't get overheated—Who am I talking to? (*She looks around the apartment and shakes her head disapprovingly. Puts bag on chair, unbuttons coat. She gets up, crosses to the coffee table, empties one ash tray into the other. Then starts to cross with the refuse into the kitchen R. when the PHONE rings. She turns and goes to the PHONE, above the coffee table. Into PHONE.*) Hello? Who?—No, he isn't. To whom am I speaking to, please? Meltzer? Martin Meltzer—No, this is Alan's mother—What?—Why should I kid about a thing like that? No, I'm positive he's not here—A message?—Wait. I'll get a pencil. (*She looks for a pencil. There is none on the table, so she runs quickly to the L. cabinet, then Upstage cabinet, turns and gestures to PHONE as if saying, "I'm coming," then to sofa table and looks frantically for a pencil. There is none to be found. She runs back R. around sofa; quickly to the PHONE.*) Go on, I'll remember. Talk fast so I could write it down as soon as you're finished—"Extremely important. Your wife just came in unexpectedly from Atlantic City and is on her way to the Hotel Croyden so Alan should be sure not to come with those certain parties."—Yes, I have it—I do—I can't repeat it to you. I'm trying to remember it— Mr. Melzer, Hotel Croyden—Yes. . . . Don't talk any more, I'm going to write it down quick. Goodbye. (*She hangs up.*) Some message. That's a book, not a message. (*She starts to look for a pencil again.*) Where's a pencil? (*She crosses R. toward counter.*) They don't have Alka-Seltzer, they're gonna have a pencil? (*The PHONE rings. She turns.*) Suddenly I'm an answering service. (*Crosses L. to PHONE, answers it.*) Hello?—No, he isn't—This is Alan's mother—why should I kid about a thing like that?—To whom am I speaking to, please?—Who?—Chickie?—That's a name?—Chickie Parker—You forgot whose hotel?—Mr. Meltzers? Where do I know that name from?—Oh, for God's sakes, he just called. With a message to Alan. Something about Atlantic City. I think he said Alan shouldn't go there—I don't know what it means either. I'm not a secretary. I'm a mother—without a pencil—The hotel?—Yes, he did mention it—I think it was the Parker—Oh, that's your name—Wait. Oh, yes. The Croyden. . . . A message for Alan? (*Cries.*) I can only try, darling— "Chickie was detained but she's on her way to the Croyden now."— Yes. You're welcome. Goodbye. (*She hangs up.*) There must be some carrying on here. (*Crosses Upstage to desk.*) Their father should only know—A businessman and a college boy and they don't have a pencil. (*She starts R. and the PHONE rings again.*) Oh, for God's sake. (*The PHONE rings again.*) All right, all right, what do you want from me? (*She rushes quickly to the PHONE and picks it up.*) Yes?—Who?—Who do you want, please?—No, he's out. This is Alan's mother—Listen, don't start that with me—Who is this?—

Connie what?—Again with a message—Miss, can't you write it down? I don't have a pencil—You what?—Yes—Yes—Yes—You're welcome—Goodbye. (*She hangs up.*) Goodbye, go home, good luck, who knows what she said? (*Sits sofa and cries.*) Who tells him to have so many phone calls?—It's disgusting. (*The PHONE rings. She screams.*) What do you want from my life? (*She just stares at the PHONE. It continues to ring.*) Oh, I'm so nauseous. (*She can't stand it any longer. She rises, picks it up, but she yells at it angrily.*) Hello?—What do you want?—Who is this?—Alan who?—Oh, Alan. . . . (*She starts to cry.*) It's Mother. (*She sits.*) What am I doing here? I'm answering your phone calls—He's out getting me a subway—I mean a taxi, No, there's no one else here—Who called?—The whole world called—First a man called—Meltzer? No, it didn't sound like that—(*The door opens and Buddy rushes in.*)

Buddy. ACT III.

In this scene opening Act Three, Buddy is utilizing a sports coat as a dancing partner. It has been three weeks since leaving home, and Buddy is a different person. Liberated for the first time from his mother and father, he has undergone a dramatic metamorphosis. Once a shy, colorless, naive person, he is now a self-assured, cocky fellow—and quite a mover with the ladies.

His actions and dialogue during the following reveal his new-found self-confidence. His dance is interrupted by a phone call from his latest acquaintance, Snow Eskanazi, a modern jazz dancer.

BUDDY

(*D. R., dancing.*) One, two, cha-cha-cha—Very good, cha-cha-cha—And turn, cha-cha-cha. (*The TELEPHONE rings on "turn."*) Answer phone, cha-cha-cha—Very good, cha-cha-cha—(*He places coat on sofa saying "Excuse me, my dear." He picks up the PHONE.*)

Hello?—Snow? (*He sits sofa.*) Don't you know you could get arrested for having such a sexy voice?—No—I'm still trying to get tickets for the Ionesco play that's opening tonight—They're supposed to call me. Then I thought we might go to the Palladium—for a little cha-cha-cha. Oh, say, could you pick me up here? It would be easier—Wonderful—42 East 63rd Street. About seven?—Make it five to. I'm only human—Goodbye. (*He hangs up, slaps his hands, and gives a little giggle of joy. Then he resumes; dances L.*) Do it right, cha-cha-cha—Tonight's the night, cha-cha-cha . . . (*The PHONE rings. He picks it up. Sits on Upstage end of coffee table.*) Hello? (*At this moment, the door opens and Alan enters. Or better, he drags in. This is not the Alan of two weeks ago. He looks bedraggled. He seems to have lost a great deal of cockiness, his self-assurance. He hangs trench coast in closet and cross D. R. to counter, picks up Fig Newton box, finds it empty, puts it down.*) Yes, it is—Yes?—Oh, wonderful—That's two tickets for tonight—Yes, I'll pick them up at the box office—In Alan Baker's name—Thank you very much. Goodbye. (*He hangs up; sees Alan.*) Oh, hi, Aly. I didn't hear you come in. (*Crossed to C.*) Gee, what a break. Your broker just got me two tickets for the Ionesco play tonight. I used your name. It is all right?

THE ODD COUPLE

(L)

Premièred March 10, 1965
at the Plymouth Theatre, New York City

Directed by Mike Nichols

CAST

Speed	Paul Dooley
Murray	Nathaniel Frey
Roy	Sidney Armus
Vinnie	John Fiedler
Oscar Madison	Walter Matthau
Felix Ungar	Art Carney
Gwendolyn Pigeon	Carole Shelley
Cecily Pigeon	Monica Evans

The action of the play takes place in an apartment on Riverside Drive in New York City.

Oscar Madison, a sports writer, is divorced from his wife Blanche and lives a life of poker and cigars in an apartment in New York City. He is undependable, unreliable, irresponsible, and one of the world's biggest slobs. During one of his traditional Friday night poker parties, Felix Ungar, a writer for CBS news, arrives in a near suicidal state because his wife Frances has given him the boot—she has finally tired of his obsessive neatness and hypochondria. Oscar invites Felix to move in, a plan doomed from the onset due to their disparate personalities.

Felix transforms the apartment from utter chaos to ordered sterility, applying his gourmet cooking and meticulousness to a degree that drives Oscar up the wall. It's an impossible, oil-and-water situation fomenting endless conflicts and a hilarious situation. As the plot unfolds, the flaws that destroyed their own marriages become manifest in the behavior of the two men, and in a classic example of transference, each take on characteristics of Frances and Blanche.

The play climaxes with an inevitable acrimonious exchange, and Felix moves out. But the dissolution is positive because both he and Oscar have grown and gained insight through their "marital" experience.

Oscar. ACT I.

A long-distance call from Oscar's wife, Blanche, has interrupted his weekly poker game. She has phoned to remind him that he is behind in his alimony payments.

Preceding speech. Speed: (*To Oscar.*) Cost you a dollar to play. You got a dollar?

OSCAR

Not after I get through talking to this lady. (*Into the PHONE. False cheerfulness.*) Hello, Blanche. How are you? . . . Err . . . Yes. . . . I have a pretty good idea why you're calling. . . . I'm a week behind with the check, right? . . . *Four* weeks? That's not possible. . . . Because it's not possible. . . . Blanche, I keep a record of every check and I *know* I'm only *three* weeks behind! . . . Blanche, I'm trying the best I can. . . . Blanche, don't threaten me with jail because it's not a threat. . . . With my expenses and my alimony, a prisoner takes home more pay than I do! . . . Very nice, in front of the kids. . . . Blanche, don't tell me you're going to have my salary attached, just say goodbye! . . . Goodbye! (*He hangs up. To Players.*) I'm eight hundred dollars behind in alimony so let's up the stakes. . . . (*Gets drink from poker table.*)

Oscar. ACT I.

Frances has ended their marriage because Felix is impossible to live with. Felix has left home in despair and has come to Oscar's apartment during his weekly poker party. After the other players have left, Oscar offers Felix his apartment and attempts to deal with his irrational, guilt-ridden behavior by telling him that he, too, is an impossible marital partner.

OSCAR

(*Up on one elbow.*) How can I help you when I can't help myself? You think *you're* impossible to live with? Blanche used to say, "What time do you want dinner?" And I'd say, "I don't know. I'm not hungry." Then at three o'clock in the morning I'd wake her up and say, "Now!" . . . I've been one of the highest paid sports writers in the East for the past fourteen years—and we saved eight and a half dollars—in pennies! I'm never home, I gamble, I burn cigar holes in the furniture, drink like a fish and lie to her every chance I get, and for our tenth wedding anniversary, I took her to see the New York Rangers-Detroit Red Wings hockey game, where she got hit with a puck. And I *still* can't understand why she left me. That's how impossible *I* am!

Oscar. ACT II. Scene ii.

It has been slightly more than two weeks since Felix moved in with Oscar, and his presence is glaringly evident. The apartment has been transformed from a hovel into Felix's immaculate conception—the place is surgically clean!

Oscar and Felix are disparate types: Oscar is a relaxed slob and Felix is a pathologically neat hypochondriac whose frailties and fastidiousness are lousing up the Friday night poker games and driving Oscar up the wall. Oscar takes Felix to task for his obsessive neatness and convinces him that they are in desperate need of female companionship. So he plans a party between them and neighboring British sisters, Gwendolyn and Cecily Pigeon.

In the following monologue at the opening of Scene Three, Oscar arrives on the eve of the party. His is in a buoyant mood, anticipating a great evening and the easy conquest of the Pigeon sisters. Felix enters during his speech and is silent and obviously disgruntled. He is

*upset that Oscar has come home late, at the end of the speech ad-
monishing him as a wife would a husband.*

*AT RISE: No one is on Stage. The dining table looks like a page out
of* House and Garden. *It's set up for dinner for four, complete with
linen tablecloth, candles and wine glasses. There is a floral center-
piece and flowers about the room, and crackers and dip on the coffee
table. There are sounds of activity in the kitchen. The front door
opens and Oscar enters with a bottle of wine in a brown paper bag,
and his jacket over his arm. He looks about gleefully as he listens to
the sounds from the kitchen. He puts the bag on the table and his
jacket over the chair, Down Right.*

OSCAR

(*Calls out. In a playful mood.*) I'm home, dear! (*He goes into his
bedroom, taking off his shirt, and comes skipping out shaving with a
cordless razor, and with a clean shirt and a tie over his arm. He is
joyfully singing as he admires the table.*) Beautiful! Just beautiful!
(*He sniffs, obviously catching the aroma from the kitchen.*) Oh, yeah.
Something wonderful is going on in that kitchen. . . . (*He rubs hands
gleefully.*) No, sir. There's no doubt about it. I'm the luckiest man on
earth. (*Puts razor into his pocket, and begins to put on shirt. Felix
enters slowly from the kitchen. He is wearing a small dish towel as
an apron. He has a ladle in one hand. He looks silently and glumly at
Oscar, crosses to the armchair and sits.*) I got the wine. (*Takes bottle
out of the bag and puts it on the table.*) Batard Montrachet. Six and a
quarter. You don't mind, do you, pussycat? We'll walk to work this
week. (*Felix sits glumly and silently.*) Hey, no kidding Felix, you did
a great job. One little suggestion? Let's come down a little with the
lights . . . (*Switches off wall brackets.*) and up very softly with the
music. (*He crosses to stereo in bookcase and picks up albums.*) What
do you think goes better with London Broil, Mancini or Sinatra?

(*Felix stares ahead.*) Felix? . . . What's the matter? (*Puts albums down.*) Something's wrong. I can tell by your conversation. (*Goes into bathroom, gets bottle of after shave lotion, comes out and puts it on.*) All right, Felix, what is it?

Oscar. ACT III.

Due to Felix's morose behavior, the evening with the Pigeon sisters was a miserable disaster. Oscar, who was salivating at the thought of slipping between the sheets with one of the girls, finds this unforgivable. The next evening, after a heated confrontation, a very angry and frustrated Oscar lays it on the line.

OSCAR

(*Moving towards him.*) I'll tell you exactly what it is. It's the cooking, cleaning and crying. . . . It's the talking in your sleep, it's the moose calls that open your cars at two o'clock in the morning. . . . I can't take it anymore, Felix. I'm crackin' up. Everything you do irritates me. And when you're not here, the things I know you're gonna do when you come in irritate me. . . . You leave me little notes on my pillow. I told you a hundred times, I can't stand little notes on my pillow. "We're all out of Corn Flakes. F.U." . . . It took me three hours to figure out that F.U. was Felix Unger. . . . It's not your fault, Felix. It's a rotten combination.

Intervening speech. Felix: I get the picture.

OSCAR (*cont'd.*)

That's just the frame. The picture I haven't even painted yet. . . . I got a typewritten list in my office of the "Ten Most Aggravating Things You Do That Drive Me Berserk." . . . But last night was the topper. Oh, that was the topper. Oh, that was the everloving lulu of all times.

Oscar. ACT III.

After Oscar's diatribe above, Felix tells Oscar that he is unreliable, undependable, irresponsible and a slob. This raises Oscar's ire to a fevered pitch, and he lets go with an even greater effusive blast.

OSCAR

(*Straightening up.*) Good. Because now I'm going to tell *you* off. . . . For six months I lived alone in this apartment. All alone in eight rooms. . . . I was dejected, despondent and disgusted. . . . Then *you* moved in. My dearest and closest friend. . . . And after three weeks of close, personal contact—I am about to have a nervous breakdown! . . . Do me a favor. Move into the kitchen. Live with your pots, your pans, your ladle and you meat thermometer. . . . When you want to come out, ring a bell and I'll run into the bedroom. (*Almost breaking down.*) I'm asking you nicely, Felix. . . . As a friend. . . . Stay out of my way! (*And he goes into the bedroom.*)

THE STAR-SPANGLED GIRL

Premièred December 21, 1966
at the Plymouth Theatre, New York City

Directed by George Axelrod

CAST

Andy Hobart	Anthony Perkins
Norman Cornell	Richard Benjamin
Sophie Rauschmeyer	Connie Stevens

The acion of the play takes place in a studio apartment in San Francisco.

Andy Hobart and Norman Cornell are financially strapped, idealistic young men who are, in spite of overwhelming odds, committed to publishing the protest magazine *Fallout*. That is, until Sophie Rauschmeyer, a sexy, athletic, all-American girl moves into their building and Norman falls obsessively in love with her—even her smell sends him into rapture. His runaway passion angers Sophie and interferes with his writing for *Fallout*. Whereas Norman is deliriously enamored of Sophie, Andy finds her a narrow-minded throwback and a distraction that threatens the life of their publication.

After Sophie loses her job thanks to Norman's outlandish behavior, Andy hires her as a means of securing Norman's productivity. But this plan is doomed because Norman cannot keep his hands off of the girl. And when Sophie reads *Fallout,* she and Andy engage in verbal crossfire generated by a diverse set of political attitudes. She sees Andy as a traitor and Communist. He views her as a provincial, narrow-minded rustic. Then, in an unexpected twist, Sophie confesses, in spite of their political dichotomy, that she finds Andy physically irresistible. Norman returns to find them kissing.

Norman, angered at finding Sophie in Andy's arms, is leaving. The threat of his departure generates a spirited argument between them, and Andy, bent upon getting out the next issue of *Fallout*, handcuffs Norman to a steam pipe. Enter Sophie. She is returning to Hunnicut, Arkansas, to train for the Olympics because she realizes that her feelings for Andy will go unrequited. Upon her departure, Andy releases Norman, announces that he is going to scrub the publication and return to Philadelphia, and confesses that he needs Sophie. Sophie, listening at the door, returns and differences are reconciled. At play's end, Sophie is back on the job dusting the apartment, Andy is concentrating on a clipboard, and Norman is flailing away at the typewriter. Sophie and Andy are an item, Norman has returned to earth, and *Fallout* will be getting out on time.

Sophie. ACT I. Scene ii.

Until Sophie moved into their building, Norman had been a literary wonk, dedicated to writing Fallout *magazine, a protest monthly published by him and his partner/roommate Andy. But since meeting Sophie,* Fallout *has become a feeble second to his efforts to woo this ultra-attractive neighbor. He has literally gone bonkers for the girl, and his efforts to capture her attention have gone to extremes. On the steps leading to her apartment he has painted "I-love-you-Sophie-Rauchmeyer." He has given her gourmet food. He has sneaked into her apartment and painted her balcony. He spies on her through his telescope. Norman is a man possessed.*

Sophie, an athletic, all-American, good girl from Arkansas, finds his behavior outrageous, and in this speech admonishes him for his improprieties.

SOPHIE

(*To Andy.*) Excuse me. (*To Norman.*) Mr. Cornell, ah have tried to be neighborly, ah have tried to be friendly and ah have tried to be cordial . . . Ah don't know what it is that you are tryin' to be . . . The first night ah was appreciative that you carried mah trunk up the stairs . . . The fact that it slipped and fell five flights and smashed into pieces was not your fault . . . Ah didn't even mind that personal message you painted on the stairs. Ah thought it was crazy, but sorta sweet . . . However, things have now gone too far . . . (*Goes down to pole table.*) Ah cannot accept gifts from a man ah hardly know . . . (*Puts basket on pole table.*) . . . Especially canned goods . . . And I read your little note. Ah can guess the gist of it even though I don't speak Italian. (*Andy sits on stool below kitchen bar.*) This has to stop, Mr. Cornell . . . Ah can do very well without you leavin' little chocolate almond Hershey bars in mah mail box . . . They melted yesterday, and now ah got three gooey letters from home with nuts in 'em . . . And ah can do without you sneakin' into mah room after ah go to work and paintin' mah balcony without tellin' me about it. Ah stepped out there yesterday and mah slippers are stilled glued to the floor . . . And ah can do without you tying big bottles of eau de Cologne to mah cat's tail. The poor thing kept swishin' it yesterday and nearly beat herself to death . . . And most of all, ah can certainly do without you watchin' me get on the bus everyday through that high-powered telescope. You got me so nervous the other day ah got on the wrong bus. In short, Mr. Cornell, and I don't want to have to say this again, *leave me ay-lone! (She turns and starts to go.)*

Sophie. ACT I. Scene ii.

Sophie's riot act has fallen on deaf ears, and Norman, thoroughly smitten, continues his outlandish advances. Sophie, frustrated and angry, threatens to call in her fiancé, First Lieutenant Burt Fenneman of the United States Marine Corps.

Andy's preceding speech. Andy: Don't look at me. I'm just an innocent bystander.

SOPHIE

So am I. Two years ago in Japan ah represented mah country in the Olympic swimming competition. In order to be a member of the Official Yewnited States Olympic swimming team, yew must be in one hundred percent perfect physical condition. That's me. Ah was one hundred per cent physically perfect. *Until* ah moved next door. From the day ah found that trail of little heart shaped peanut brittles leading from mah door to his door, ah have been a nervous wreck . . . Not only is it difficult to keep up with mah swimming, but ah'm afraid to take a bath. Ah have found that when ah brush mah hair, mah hair falls out. And the ones that fall out have not been replaced by new ones . . . Ah am twenty-three years old and that man is start-ing me on the road to total baldness. Ah intend to get married while ah still have a full head of hair left. (*She goes to the door.*) Ah am now going to have a dinner of good, basic American food, clean mah apartment and get ten hours sleep. If ah see him sittin' in that big tree outside mah window again, strummin' that ukulele and singin' those Spanish love songs, ah'm gonna call for the United States Marines. (*She exits and slams the door.*)

Andy. ACT I. Scene ii.

Sophie enters screaming. Norman is in her apartment mopping her kitchen floor. This is too much, she has had it, she want this nut out of her life. When she threatens to call the police, Andy, who knows that Norman's confinement would jeopardize the publication of Fallout, *attempts to reason with her.*

ANDY

Why did I ask? I'll try to explain what we do. (*Points to sign above bulletin board on L. Wall.*) This is our credo, "A Remedy for a Sick Society." . . . (*Goes L. above pole table.*) We're not doctors, we're diagnosticians. We point to the trouble spots. I'm the editor and pub-lisher. It's my job to get it printed and sold. Norman is our staff. He is fourteen of the best writers around today. Every word, from cover to cover, is his. Besides Norman Cornell, he is sometimes Abbott Kellerman, Professor O. O. Pentergast, Gaylord Heyerdahl, Jose Batista, Madame Pundit Panjab, Doctor Sidney Kornheiser, Major General Wylie Krutch and Akruma Oogwana . . . The kid is versatile . . . Now we may use assumed names, but we believe in what we write and in what we publish. (*Gets copy of* Fallout *from a pile of magazines under the L. end of desk.*) When you go back to your room, I would like you to read last month's issue, and then I want you to tell me if you think we've spent three years and every penny we have in the world for nothing. (*Goes R., with magazine, D. of Sophie, to below C. table.*) Tell me if the things we protest against every month in *Fallout* aren't the things you protest against every day in your everyday life. (*Sophie starts to interrupt.*) We have a modest business here, Miss Rauschmeyer. We don't make much money. If we sell every magazine we print each months, we make just enough to buy a new typewriter ribbon so we can get out the next months' issue. But we stay alive. And we love every minute of it. And we'll continue doing it as long as there is an angry breath in our body and as long as there is one single iota of corruption left in our society that's worth protesting about. (*Sophie makes a move to interrupt.*) But Miss Rauschmeyer, unless you smile at that talented lunatic in there and say "Thank you for your little Budapest sausages" . . . one of the great organs of the free press will disappear from the American scene . . . (*There is a pause for her reaction.*)

Andy. ACT II. Scene ii.

Due to Norman's pestering her at work, Sophie has been fired from her job as swimming instructor at the YWCA. In order to placate her, Andy engages Sophie at her former salary. Ostensibly, she will act as their secretary, but her primary function is to be nice to Norman and smile at him occasionally so that he will write at peak performance, an arrangement that proves to be quite unsatisfactory because Norman will not leave Sophie alone.

Sophie, an ultra-right, countrified girl, has read Fallout *and is appalled by its "anti-American" point of view. She chastises Andy for his involvement with the magazine and accuses him of being a Communist, fascist, and traitor, full of deceit and treachery. He retaliates as follows:*

ANDY

(*Slams door. Comes D. to bottom step.*) Okay, I'm deceitful and treacherous. And *you* are provincial and old-fashioned, antiquated, unrealistic, unimaginative, unenlightened, uninformed, and unbelievably unable to understand anything that isn't under water . . . (*Sophie rises.*) Your big trouble in life is that you were born a hundred and fifty years too late. You should have been at Bunker Hill loading muskets, raising flags and waiting for the British to show up with the whites of their eyes. Well, you may be shocked to learn that this is 1966 and this country has a whole new set of problems. But you wouldn't know about that because I don't think you're a real person of flesh and blood with feelings and sensitivities. I don't think you could be capable of having a genuine emotional attachment for another human being unless it was first passed by Congress and amended to the Constitution and painted red, white and blue. (*Goes to L. of pole table.*) If you've been listening carefully, Miss Rauschmeyer, I have just made a point.

Sohpie. ACT III.

Even though Sophie is repulsed by Andy's attitude and politics, she tells him that she finds him physically irresistible. She pursues him, he resists, but ultimately they embrace. Norman, finding them in each other's arms, announces that he is abandoning Fallout *and leaving to take a job as a writer for the Associated Press. After a heated quarrel and quasi fight, Andy handcuffs Norman to a steam pipe and threatens to hold him there until Andy completes the upcoming issue of their magazine.*

At this point Sophie enters and announces that she is returning to Arkansas and foregoing her marriage plans because of her unreciprocated feelings for Andy. But before leaving, she imparts the following words of admonition:

SOPHIE

(*To Andy.*) Well, ah'll tell you anyway. You're right. Ah may be provincial and old-fashioned. Ah may believe in a lot of things like patriotism and the Constitution because that's the way ah was brought up, and that's the way ah feel. The trouble with you is, you can't feel. You can't feel, you can't see, you can't hear and oh, boy, *you can't smell. All* you can do is think. But until you learn to use all those wonderful gadgets that nature has given you, you are only one-fifth of a man. Unfortunately by the time you get them all workin' and realize you are crazy about me, ah will be back home in mah high school gymnasium gettin' in shape for next year's Olympics. If you want mah advice, ah suggest you take those pennies and visit an eye, ear, nose and throat man. (*Starts for door.*) And maybe you ought to see a dentist too. Because mah former fiancé, not happy with the recent turn of events, is on his way over here to separate your teeth from your face.

Sophie. ACT III.

As an addendum to the speech above, Sophie offers this parting shot:

SOPHIE

(*Goes to stairs leading to front door.*) That's right, ah'm leavin'! Ah'm leavin'! Back to Hunnicut. And startin' tomorrow ah'm gonna swim a mile every day from now until next summer. (*Comes down steps toward C. table.*) Every American has to do what he does best for his country, and ah-can-swim! Ah'm gonna swim the United States right into a gold medal and this time ah'm gonna beat the livin' nose plugs offa that little fat girl from the desert. (*She picks up the PHONE off the floor.*) I'm usin' your phone one more time. (*She dials.*) Gimme Western Union! (*To Andy.*) And what you did to blacken America's good name with your protestin' magazine, ah will whitewash with mah backstroke down in Mexico City. (*Into the PHONE.*) Ah'd like to send a telegram, please. To Mr. Andrew Hobart, 217, Chestnut Hill, San Francisco. (*She looks at Andy.*) . . . Dear Mr. Hobart. Whether you like it or not, ah pledge allegiance to the flag of the United States of America . . . and to the Republic for which if stands, one nation, under God, indivisible, with Liberty and Justice for all . . . Sign that "A Patriot" and send it collect. (*She hangs up, puts the PHONE back on the floor and exits with a flourish.*)

Andy. ACT III.

Upon Sophie's departure, Andy admits defeat and announces that he is folding the magazine.

ANDY

Murder! I'm going to commit cold-blooded murder right in this room. (*Rises and goes L.*) I'm going to kill the only thing in this world that really means anything to me—my magazine. (*He takes the key and unlocks Norman's handcuffs.*) There! Go on, you're free. Now get out of here and let me bury the body. (*He goes to the bulletin board while Norman goes C. Andy rips down the credo sign and breaks it over his knee.*) Maybe you were right. Maybe you were both right. Maybe I am crazy, Maybe it was lunatic to try to hold on to one tiny, not very important, insignificant little voice-in-the-wilderness against such overwhelming odds as a girl-smelling mental case and a wetback Martha Washington. (*Picks up magazines from pole table and takes them R. to the duffel bag on the sofa. Puts magazines into bag.*) I'm sure she'll be very happy now. America is safe tonight. In tribute, tomorrow Howard Johnson's will add another flavor. (*Throws duffel bag on floor.*) She's won, don't you see that, she's won. Divide and conquer, that's the way they do it. Well, we're divided and we're conquered. The war is over and we've surren- dered. In reparations, she gets the Polish corridor, the free city of Danzig, three outfielders, two turtle doves and a partridge in a pear tree. (*He collapses into chair R. of table.*)

PLAZA SUITE
(L)

Premièred February 14, 1968
at the Plymouth Theatre, New York City

Directed by Mike Nichols

CAST

"Visitor from Mamaroneck"

Bellhop	Bob Balaban
Karen Nash	Maureen Stapleton
Sam Nash	George C. Scott
Waiter	Jose Ocasio
Jean McCormack	Claudette Nevins

"Visitor from Hollywood"

Waiter	Jose Ocasio
Jesse Kiplinger	George C. Scott
Muriel Tate	Maureen Stapleton

"Visitor from Forest Hills"

Norma Hubley	Maureen Stapleton
Roy Hubley	George C. Scott
Bordern Isler	Bob Balaban
Mimsey Hubley	Claudett Nevins

Plaza Suite is constituted of three one-act plays that take place in Suite 719 at the Plaza Hotel, New York City.

"The Visitor from Mamaroneck."

While Karen and Sam Nash are having their house painted, they take a suite at the Plaza until the work is completed. Karen, sensing an opportunity to revitalize romantic juices, books Suite 719, the room she and Sam had occupied on their wedding night. But Sam is not romantically inclined. Sadly, Karen's desire for intimacy is dashed, and the evening becomes one of verbal fencing and petty bickering during which the fragile state of their marriage surfaces.

Sam's secretary, Jean, arrives with important papers to sign. She is young, attractive and slim. They confer, and business matters necessitate that Sam return to his office that evening. When Karen asks Sam if he is having an affair with Jean, he vehemently denies it, but, upon further probing, admits to the relationship. Karen feigns understanding, but underneath she is hurting and wishes to salvage their marriage of twenty-three years. She begs Sam not to go to his office, where he will be working late with Jean, but Sam, after vacillating, tells her that he has to go.

Karen. ACT I.

Karen bids the bellhop farewell and orders up champagne and hors d'oeuvres. She is looking forward with great anticipation to Sam's arrival and the possibility of long-overdue intimacy.

KAREN

Thank you, dear . . . and take my advice. Don't rush . . . but look around for another job. (*The Boy nods and exits. Karen crosses to the bedroom, and looks at herself in the full-length mirror on the closet door. She takes off hat and puts it on the dresser.*) You are definitely some old lady. (*She crosses to the PHONE on night table next to bed, takes it and sits on bed, still wearing her mink coat.*) Room service,

please. (*She groans as she bends over to take of galoshes.*) Ohhhhh
. . . (*Into the PHONE.*) No, operator. I was groaning to myself . . .
(*Taking off her coat.*) Hello, room service? . . . Listen, room service,
this is Mrs. Sam Nash in Suite 719 . . . I would like a nice, cold bottle
of champagne . . . That sounds good, is it French? . . . Fine . . . with
two glasses and a tray of assorted hors d'oeuvres . . . but listen, room
service, I don't want any anchovies . . . They always give you
anchovy patties with the hors d'oeuvres and my husband doesn't eat
anchovies and I hate them so don't give me any anchovies . . .
Instead of the anchovies, give me some extra smoked salmon or you
can split them up . . . half smoked salmon and half caviars . . . That's
right. Mrs. Nash. 719 . . . No anchovies . . . (*She hangs up.*) They'll
give me anchovies. (*She puts PHONE back on night table.*) Look at
that. No more Savoy-Plaza. (*Starts to take off galoshes again. The
TELEPHONE rings. There is one in each room. She gets up and
picks up the one next to bed.*) Hello . . . (*The PHONE in the living
room rings again. Hastily she hangs up the bedroom PHONE and
rushes to answer it.*) Hello? . . . Oh, Sam. Where are you? . . . Good.
Come up. I'm here . . . What room do you think? . . . 719 . . .
Remember? 719? Suite 719? . . . That's right! (*She hangs up.*) He
doesn't remember . . . (*She rushes to Bendel box and takes out a
sheer negligee. She crosses to mirror on closet door, and looks at
herself with the negligee in front of her. She is not completely en-
chanted. The TELEPHONE rings. She puts down the negligee and
rushes to living room to answer it.*) Hello . . . (*The PHONE in the
bedroom rings again. She hastily hangs up the living room PHONE
and rushes to answer it.*) Hello? . . . Oh, hello, Miss McCormack . . .
No, he's not, dear. He's on his way up. Yes, I will . . . It's not important, is it? . . . Well, he seemed so tired lately, I was hoping he
wouldn't have to think about work tonight. (*Glancing down at her
feet.*) Oh, my God, I still have my galoshes on . . . All right, I'll tell
him to call. Yes, when he comes in. Goodbye. (*She hangs up and*

quickly bends over in an effort to remove her galoshes. She is having difficulty. The DOORBELL rings.) Oh, dammit. (*Calls out*.) Just a minute! (*The DOORBELL rings again. She is having much trouble with the right galosh*.) You had to wear galoshes today, right? (*She pulls her right galosh off but her shoe remains in it. The DOORBELL rings impatiently*.) Oh, for God's sakes . . . (*She tries to pull her shoe out of the galosh but it is embedded in there*.) All right, all right, I'm coming . . . (*She throws down the galosh with shoe still in it and "limps" across the room in one galosh and her stockinged foot. She crosses into living room*.) Look at this, my twenty-fourth anniversary. (*She "Limps" to the door and opens it. Sam Nash stands there. Sam has just turned fifty but has made every effort to conceal it. He is trim, impeccable neat. His clothes are well-tailored, although a bit on the junior executive side. He carries an attaché case, a fine leather Gucci product. Everything about Sam is measured, efficient, economic. Smile warmly*.) Hello, Sam.

"Visitor from Hollywood."

While in New York on business, big-time movie producer Jesse Kiplinger phones his high-school sweetheart, Muriel Tate. He is a jaded denizen of the Hollywood scene and disillusioned with the women in his life. In Muriel he looks forward to an afternoon of harmless sex with a woman still demure and unaffected. But reality proves otherwise. Muriel, a heavy drinker, locked in an unhappy marriage, is far from the sweet innocent he knew at Tenafly High.

Jesse. ACT II.

While playing cat and mouse in an attempt to get Muriel into bed, Jesse tells of his movie obsession, his success, and his failure with women.

JESSE

Yes, I'll tell you. Why did I call you yesterday? After seventeen years? Okay, let's start with, "Yes, I'm a Famous Hollywood Producer. Yes, I never made a picture that lost money. Yes, I got that magic touch, call it talent, whatever you want, I don't know." . . . The fact is, ever since I was old enough to sneak into the Ridgewood Theater in Tenafly, I've been a movie nut. (*Getting up, stands by sofa.*) Not only have I seen every Humphrey Bogart movie he ever made at least eight times, I now own a print of all those pictures. Why do you think I was so crazy to buy his house? (*Moves slowly to window.*) So I went to Hollywood and was very lucky and extremely smart and presto, I became a producer. (*Unobtrusively pulls down the shade.*) I love making movies. Some are good, some are bad, most of them are fun. I hope I can continue doing it for the next fifty years. That's one half of my life. The other half is that in the last fourteen years I've been married three times—to three of the worst bitches you'd ever want to meet. (*Gets bottle of Vodka and glass from bar.*)

Jesse. ACT II.

He continues his outpouring about his unsuccessful marriages. (In the interest of greater duration, this speech may be coupled with the preceding.)

JESSE

(*Moves to Muriel.*) What happened . . . I gave them love, I gave them a home, I gave them a beautiful way of life—and the three bitches took me for every cent I got. (*Refills her glass, then sits on floor by armchair.*) But I don't even care about the money, screw it—excuse me, Muriel. What hurts is that they took the guts out of me—They were phony, unfaithful, all of them. Did you know I caught my first wife, Delores, in bed with a jockey? A jockey! (*Indicates size, hold-*

ing hand a foot off the floor.) Do you know what it does to a man's self-respect to find his wife in the sack with a four-foot-eight shrimp, weighs a hundred and twelve pounds? . . . But as I said before, screw it. Tell me if I'm shocking you, Muriel. (*Refills his own drink*.)

Jesse. ACT II.

In Muriel he sees an uncorrupted, pure woman. She represents a pristine island floating in a polluted sea.

JESSE

(*Getting up, replenishes her drink*.) Muriel, forget the Los Angeles Rams . . . (*Putting bottle and his glass down on the console table, he crosses behind sofa*.) Listen to what I'm saying to you. I am in a very bad way. I've been through three hellish, miserable marriages. I don't want to go that route again. I'm losing my faith and belief that there is anything left that resembles an uncorrupt woman . . . (*Sighs*.) So last week my mother, who still gets the Tenafly newspaper, shows me a picture of the PTA annual outing at Palisades this year and who is there on the front page, coming in first in the Mother and Daughter Potato Race, (*Leans in to Muriel over side arm of couch*.) looking every bit as young and lovely and as sweet as she did seventeen years ago, was my last salvation . . . Muriel Tate. (*Gradually moving to bedroom door*.) That's why I had to see you, Muriel. Just to talk to you, to have a drink, to spend five minutes, to affirm my faith that there *are* decent women in this world . . . even if it's only one . . . even if you're the last of a dying species . . . if somebody like you exists, Muriel . . . then maybe there's still somebody for me . . . *That's* why I called you yesterday. (*Jesse has finished his speech. He is somewhat spent, emotionally. He moves to bed and sits*.)

"Visitor from Forest Hills."

On her wedding day, Mimsey Hubley has locked herself in the bathroom. Downstairs in the Green Room awaits groom Borden Eisler and his family along with sixty-eight guests, nine waiters, a photographer, and four musicians—not to mention a fortune in spoiling hors d'oeuvres. Mother and father stall, but Mimsey is intractable. She remains locked in the bathroom as Norma and Roy Hubley grow more frustrated and panicked with each passing second.

After a seemingly interminable period during which Roy nearly breaks his arm, falls from a seven-story ledge, rips his rented tux, and Norma rips her hose and nearly succumbs to anxiety, Mimsey emerges from the john at her fiancé's terse command, "Cool it." Mimsey's reluctance to leave the bathroom stemmed from a fear for what she and Borden might become—a disgruntled, bickering couple. Like her parents.

Norma. ACT III.

In this speech, which opens the scene, Norma phones the Green Room, stalls the groom's father, and frantically summons husband Roy. She is not only in a state of near panic due to Mimsey refusing to leave the bathroom, she also dreads breaking the news to Roy.

NORMA
(*On the PHONE.*) Hello? . . . Hello, Operator? . . . Can I have the Blue Room, please . . . The Blue Room . . . Is there a Pink Room? . . . I want the Hubley-Eisler wedding . . . The Green Room, that's it. Thank you . . . Could you please hurry, operator, it's an emergency . . . (*Looks at bathroom nervously. Paces back and forth.*) Hello? . . . Who's this? . . . Mr. Eisler . . . It's Norma Hubley . . . No, everything's fine . . . Yes, we're coming right down . . . (*She is*

smiling and trying to act as pleasant and as calm as possible.) Yes, you're right, it certainly *is* the big day . . . Mr. Eisler, is my husband there? . . . Would you, please? . . . Oh! Well, I'd like to wish you the very best of good luck too . . . Borden's a wonderful boy . . . Well, they're *both* wonderful kids . . . No, no. She's a calm as a cucumber . . . That's the younger generation, I guess . . . Yes, everything seems to be going along beautifully . . . Absolutely beautifully . . . Oh, thank you. (*Her husband has obviously just come on the other end because the expression on her face changes violently and she screams a rasping whisper filled with doom. Sitting on bed*.) Roy? You'd better get up here right away, we're in big trouble . . . Don't ask questions, just get up here . . . I hope you're not drunk because I can't handle this alone . . . Don't say anything. Just smile and walk leisurely out the door . . . and then get the hell up here as fast as you can. (*She hangs up, putting the PHONE back on night table. She crosses to the bathroom and then puts her head up against the door. Aloud through bathroom door*.) All right, Mimsey, you father's on his way up. Now, I want you to come out of that bathroom and get married. (*There is no answer*.) Do you hear me? . . . I've had enough of this nonsense . . . Unlock that door! (*That's about the end of her authority. She wilts and almost pleads*.) Mimsey, darling, please come downstairs and get married, you know your father's temper . . . I know what you're going through now, sweetheart, you're just nervous . . . Everyone goes through that on their wedding day . . . It's going to be all right, darling. You love Borden and he loves you. You're both going to have a wonderful future. So please come out of the bathroom! (*She listens, there is no answer*.) Mimsey, if you don't care about your life, think about mine. Your father'll kill me. (*The front DOORBELL rings. Norma looks off nervously, moves to other side of the bed*.) Oh, God, he's here! . . . Mimsey! Mimsey, please, spare me this . . . If you want, I'll have it annulled next week, but please come out and get married! (*No answer from bathroom, but the front DOORBELL rings impatiently.*) All right. I'm letting your father in. And heaven help the three of us!

Norma. ACT III.

In an attempt to extricate Mimsey, Roy has crawled out of their seventh-floor window and is inching his way along the ledge toward the bathroom. Norma (by now nearly a basket case), fearful for her husband's life, does her best to assure Mr. Eisler, the groom's father, that everything is under control.

NORMA

(*Bemoaning her fate.*) He'll kill himself. He'll fall and kill himself, that's the way my luck's been going all day. (*She staggers away from the window and leans on the bureau.*) I'm not going to look. I'll just wait until I hear a scream. (*The TELEPHONE rings and Norma screams in fright.*) Aggghhh! . . . I thought it was him . . . (*She crosses to the PHONE by the bed. The TELEPHONE rings again.*) Oh, God, what am I going to say? (*She picks it up.*) Hello? . . . Oh, Mr. Eisler. Yes, we're coming . . . My husband's getting Mimsey now . . . We'll be right down. Have some more hors d'oeuvres . . . Oh, thank you. It certainly *is* the happiest day of my life. (*She hangs up.*) No, I'm going to tell him I've got a husband dangling over Fifty-ninth Street. (*As she crosses back to the opened window, a sudden torrent of RAIN begins to fall. As she gets to the window and sees it.*) I knew it! I knew it! It had to happen . . . (*She gets closer to the window and tries to look out.*) Are you all right, Roy? . . . Roy? (*There's no answer.*) He's not all right, he fell. (*She staggers into the bedroom.*) He fell, he fell, he fell, he fell . . . He's dead, I know it. (*She collapses onto the armchair.*) He's laying there in a puddle in front of Trader Vic's . . . I'm passing out. This time I'm really passing out! (*She passes out on the chair, legs and arms spread-eagled. The*

DOORBELL rings, she jumps right up.) I'm coming! I'm coming! Help me, whoever you are, help me! (*She rushes through the bedroom into the living room and to the front door*.) Oh, please, somebody, help me, please!

Roy. ACT III.

After a failed attempt to reach Mimsey by skirting the ledge seven floors above the street, Roy has reentered the building through an adjacent window. He is wet, disheveled, and furious.

Preceding speech. Norma: (*Stopping him below bed*.) Don't yell at her. Don't get her more upset.

ROY

(*Turning back to her*.) Don't get her *upset*? I'm hanging seven stories from a gargoyle in a pouring rain and you want me to worry about *her*? . . . You know what she's doing in there? She's playing with her false eyelashes. (*Moves to bathroom door*.) I'm out there fighting for my life with pigeons and she's playing with eyelashes . . . (*Crossing back to Norma*.) I already made up my mind. The minute I get my hands on her, I'm gonna kill her. (*Moves back to door*.) Once I show them the wedding bills, no jury on earth would convict me . . . And if by some miracle she survives, let there be no talk of weddings . . . She can go into a convent. (*Slowly moving back to Norma below bed*.) Let her become a librarian with thick glasses and a pencil in her hair, I'm not paying for anymore canceled weddings . . . (*Working himself up into a frenzy, he rushes to the table by the armchair and grabs up some newspapers*.) Now get her out of there or I start to burn these newspapers and smoke her out.

Roy. ACT III.

In another mishap that heightens Roy's anger and frustration, Norma has just broken her diamond ring banging on the bathroom door. This is the last straw, and Roy denounces his wife, daughter, and the entire wedding with an outburst of intense hostility.

ROY

(*Yells through door.*) Hey, you with the false eyelashes! (*Getting up and moving to door.*) . . . You want to see a broken diamond ring? You want to see eighteen hundred dollars worth of crushed baguets? . . . (*He grabs Norma's hand and holds it to keyhole.*) Here! Here! *This* is a worthless family heirloom—(*Kicks the door.*) and *this* is a diamond bathroom door. (*Controlling himself. To Norma.*) Do you know what I'm going to do now? Do you have any idea? (*Norma puts her hand to her mouth, afraid to hear. Roy moves away from the door to the far side of bed.*) I'm going to wash my hands of the entire Eisler-Hubley wedding. You can take all the Eislers and all the hors d'oeuvres and go to Central Park and have an eight thousand dollar picnic . . . (*Stops and turns back to Norma.*) I'm going down to the Oak Room with my broken arm, with my drenched rented ripped suit—and I'm gonna get blind! . . . I don't mean drunk, I mean totally blind . . . (*Erupting with great vehemence.*) because I don't want to see you or your crazy daughter again, if I live to be a thousand.

LAST of the RED HOT LOVERS

Premièred December 28, 1969
at the Eugene O'Neill Theatre, New York City

Directed by Robert Moore

CAST

Barney Cashman	James Coco
Elaine Navazio	Linda Lavin
Bobbi Michele	Marcia Rodd
Jeanette Fisher	Doris Roberts

The action of the the play takes place in an apartment in New York's East Thirties.

Barney Cashman is the middle-aged proprietor of a fish restaurant in New York City. He is a devoted husband of twenty-three years, gentle, kind, and decent. His life has been exemplary. But at age forty-seven he has awakened to the fact that his life has also been adventureless and boring. Threatened by thoughts of his mortality, he has decided to break the pattern of his bland existence by having an affair. So he arranges assignations to take place in his mother's apartment while she is away doing volunteer work at Mount Sinai. But each is doomed by character conflicts and the fact that Barney is essentially a moral person, a good man who, in spite of his desperation, is not comfortable with cheating on his wife.

His first encounter is with Elaine Navazio, a tough-talking realist who is no stranger to infidelity. Barney is clumsy and reticent. Elaine is bold and impatient and quickly tires of his furtiveness and inexperience. The second liaison is between Barney and Bobbi Michele, a young, dope-smoking, promiscuous basket case whose incessant ramblings reveal her aberrant lifestyle. The wide moral and generational gap between them results in another failed rendezvous. The final episode involves Jeanette Fisher, a personal friend of Barney and his wife who is morbidly depressed and negative due to her husband's affair. Her depression hangs over the proceedings like a wet shroud, once again dooming the assignation.

Elaine. ACT I.

Barney, shocked by Elaine's "callous" attitude with respect to sex, has become self-righteous and a bit preachy. Elaine—who is totally honest, guiltless, and open regarding her sexual appetite—lashes back.

ELAINE

You hypocrite! You soul-searching, fingersmelling, hypocritical son of a bitch! Who are you to tell anybody how to go through life? What would you have done if I came here all fluttery and blushing and "Ooh, Mr. Cashman, don't put your hand there, I'm a married woman?" Were you going to tell me how much you respect me, admire me and, at the moment of truth, even love me? You know damn well tomorrow you'd be back behind that counter opening clams and praying to Christ I'd never come back in your restaurant. And you know something? That's the way it should be. Forgive me for the terrible, sinful thing I'm about to say but I happen to like the pure physical act of making love. It warms me, it stimulates me and it makes me feel like a women—but that's another ugly story. That's what I came up here for and that's what you were expecting. But don't give me, "When I was nine years old my mother ran off with the butcher and I've been looking for someone to love me ever since." I don't know your problems and I don't care. Keep you savory swordfish succotash stories to yourself. No one really cares about anything or anyone in this world except himself, and there's only one way to get through with your sanity. If you can't taste it, touch it, or smell it, forget it! If you want a copy of that speech, send fifty cents and a self-addressed envelope—

Barney. ACT I.

After Elaine's diatribe—when she attempts to leave—Barney shoves her into a chair and demands that she listen. He is in a state of emotional foment, shaking with anger.

This speech presents the crux of Barney's need for an affair—the sense of his own mortality. Time is running out on a man who has lived a good but uneventful, boring, ordinary existence. Now, for just one golden moment, he wants to break the pattern and live!

This unbridled verbal torrent expresses a universal frustration with pathos and humor .

BARNEY

Just sit there! Don't talk, don't cough, don't even breathe. Just sit there and shut up until I tell you you can go. If I get nothing else from you this afternoon it's going to be your undivided goddamned attention! Excuse me! (*Crosses to the bottle, pours himself a drink, and gulps it down. She looks at him incredulously but silently. He does not look at her.*) I'm sure it will come as no great shock to you, but you are the first "attempted" extramarital affair for me in twenty-three years of marriage. I've never even kissed another woman. In twenty-three years. I got married to my high-school sweetheart—and when have you heard that expression last—at the age of twenty-four, having gone steady with her since I was sixteen. And how many experiences with other women do you think I've had prior to getting married? . . . One! I had one shot at it. When I was eighteen my brother took me to an apartment in Newark, New Jersey, where I consorted with a forty-four-year-old woman who greeted me lying naked on a brass bed reading a newspaper. It cost me seven dollars and I threw up all night. I don't smoke, I don't gamble, and you've had more to drink this afternoon than I've had in my whole life. I've never had a car accident, never had a fistfight, never had a broken bone, never had a temperature over a hundred and two. . . . Life has not only been very kind to me, it goes out of its way to ignore me . . . I've got three kids I'm very proud of, a house I've worked very hard for and a wife who is not extraordinary, not what you would call an exciting, vivacious woman, but one who is kind, considerate, devoted and that I happen to love. So why after twenty-three years do I write my mother's address on the back of a check, buy a bottle of Scotch with two glass and pray to God I never get caught? Why? I'll tell you why . . . I don't know. I've never had the urge before. . . . Not true. I started getting the urge about five years ago. Two years ago seriously. About a year ago I decided to give in to it, and the last six months conscientiously. I'm forty-seven years old and for the first time in my life I think about dying. The thought of death has now become a part of my life. I read the obituaries every day just for the satisfaction of not seeing my name there. I constantly think about how it's going to come and how I'm going to bear up to it. Do you know I even practice dying? I lie in bed at night trying to feel myself slipping away . . . and then I let my head drop off to the side . . . and then I let out my last gasp of air . . . and then I go in and take two sleeping pills because I'm up the rest of the night scared out of my wits. But it's inevitable, it's going to happen someday, maybe sooner than I think. And I ask myself, "Have you enjoyed it, Barney? Was it really a terrific forty-seven years?" And you know what my answer is? "Well, I wouldn't say terrific. It was nice." . . . The sum total of my existence is nice. I will go to my grave having led a nice life. And I will have a nice funeral and they will bury me in my nice blue suit. And my wife will weep for me and mourn for me and in six months she will marry another nice fellow . . . maybe even give him my brown sports jacket. And I wouldn't condemn her for it. It's the natural order of things. Life must go on. . . . But while it's going on, shouldn't it be better than just "nice"? Shouldn't there be something else besides opening the restaurant eleven o'clock every morning?

Shouldn't there be something better than those three weeks every August in Saratoga Springs where I stand in a pool with fifty fat middle-aged people, wishing I were home opening the restaurant at eleven o'clock in the morning? Couldn't I just once give in to my fantasies, my secret dreams, experiencing things, emotions, stimulants I've never experienced before? . . . I wanted to know what it was like with another woman. Would I be successful, would she like me, would I like to touch her? A thousand questions that I'd never know the answer to if suddenly my name were in the obituary column tomorrow morning. So I decided to indulge myself, just once. I don't pretend I'm being fair to my wife. If she indulged herself the same way I'd never forgive her. So I started looking around . . . and, I promise you, with all the intentions of having one affair, one day of pleasure and that's all. But if it was just going to be one day I wanted it to be memorable—an experience so rewarding and fulfilling that it would last me the rest of my life . . . not cheap, not sordid. And then I'd go back to opening the restaurant at eleven o'clock in the morning—but knowing that for one brief afternoon I had changed the pattern of my life, and for once I didn't just exist—I lived!

Elaine. ACT I.

She responds after listening to Barney's outpouring, hinting at the tragic state of her formative years and rightfully chastising him for his naiveté and grandiose illusions. She bids him farewell, praying that there's a cigarette machine in the lobby. Upon her departure, Barney swears that he will never, never repeat the episode.

ELAINE

No, listen, it was terrifically entertaining. I really enjoyed it. There's one or two reasons, though, why I couldn't feel too sympathetic for the hero. . . . In the first place, there is a very good possibility that

that forty-four-year-old woman in Newark, New Jersey, was my mother. That'll give you some idea of my background. In the second place, any man who expects to have a beautiful, memorable and enchanting day of honest love with a woman he picks up in a fish restaurant is either sexually retarded or a latent idiot! And in the third place, no one gives a good crap about you dying because a lot of people discovered it ahead of you. We're all dying, Mr. Cashman. As a matter of fact, I myself passed away about six months ago. I'm just hanging around to clean up some business affairs. . . . Together, Barney, we blew one of the very few free afternoons we have allotted to us in this life. But I'm not putting the blame on you. It serves me right. If I had a craving for corned beef and cabbage I'd be in some big Irishman's apartment right now having the time of my life. . . . *C'est la vie!* (*At the door.*) Good luck, Barney, in your quest for the Impossible Dream. (*Opens the door.*) Oh, please, God, let there be a machine in the lobby. . . . (*And she is gone.*)

Barney. ACT III.

After his failed encounter with a sexually depraved dingbat, Barney welcomes Jeanette, a close personal acquaintance of both he and his wife. In this speech, which opens Act Three, Barney welcomes her and attempts to put her at ease. But Jeanette, a hopelessly depressed middle-aged woman, immediately throws a wet blanket over the proceedings.

BARNEY

(*With some sincerity.*) Hello, Jeanette! (*Extends his hand and leads her into the room, closing the door behind him.*) Any trouble finding the place? (*She shakes here head "no."*) It's not raining yet, is it? (*She shakes her head "no" again.*) Good. Good. (*He starts to walk around to her front but she turns away, her back to him, not looking at anything in particular.*) Jeanette, there's nothing wrong, is there? (*Another wordless shake of her head. He goes over and takes her hand.*) Well, then, come here and sit down. . . . Hey, come on, Jeanette, look at me. (*She finally lifts head and looks at him.*) You okay? (*She finally manages a small smile and nods "yes."*) Come here. (*He leads her to the sofa; they both sit.*) Listen, there's no sense in denying this is a little awkward. But that's why I respect you, Jeanette. If you weren't nervous, if you just barged in here, cold and callous like some women could, or if you were some—some *nut* I met in the park, that would be one thing. But you're not, Jeanette. You are the only one in our circle, the *only* one of Thelma's friends that I have ever had any respect of feeling for. That's why I was so happy the other night when we were having dinner at your place, when you indicated to me—(*Suddenly Jeanette begins to sob quietly.*) Oh, Jeanette, don't. It's all right. (*She grabs a handkerchief out of her pocketbook and cries quietly into it.*) Hey, come on, Jeanette. None of that now. . . . (*She is sobbing. He starts to put his arm around her shoulder to comfort her.*) Listen, it's all right. It's just me. Barney. (*She pushes him away. He looks around, not knowing what to do.*) Jeanette, you're not going to sit here crying until five o'clock, are you? . . . *Are* you? (*Jeanette suddenly jumps up and rushes into the bathroom, still sobbing. Barney gets up.*) Jeanette! . . . Jeanette? (*But she's in the bathroom. He goes over and listens to her through the door. Then he walks away and throws his arms up in dismay.*) Oh, Christ! (*He talks to himself.*) Boy, can you pick 'em! Can you pick 'em!

Jeanette. ACT III.

Jeanette's downer attitude stems from the fact that her husband is having an affair with a one of her best friends, an infidelity that has left her morbid, negative, depressed and without the ability to taste food.

JEANETTE

You know what my proof is? He told me. Two o'clock in the morning he leans over, taps me on the shoulder and says, "I've had an affair with Charlotte Korman." Who asked him? When he tapped me on the shoulder in the middle of the night I thought he wanted *me!* You know what it is to wake up from a sound sleep with no eyelashes and a dry mouth and hear that your husband is getting it from a woman you're not allowed to see for lunch? And you know why he told me, Barney? He ex-plained it to me. We're living in a new guiltless society. You can do anything you want as long as you're honest about it. Aren't we lucky to be living in such a civilized age? In the old days I would have gone to my grave *ignorant* of the wonderful and beautiful knowledge that my husband was spending his afternoons humping Charlotte Korman! . . . When he told me, I didn't say a word. I went down to the kitchen and made myself a cream cheese and jelly sandwich on date-nut bread. And that was the last time in eight months that I tasted food. . . . I estimate, going four times a week, I should be through with Doctor Margolies in another year. And then, when we both think I'm ready, I'm going to get in my car and drive off the Verrazano Bridge. In the meantime, I'm very depressed. Excuse me, Barney. Nothing personal, but I don't think we're going to have our affair.

Barney. ACT III.

Jeanette's morbidity is absolute. And her view of humankind is totally negative—there is no one left on earth who is gentle, loving, and decent. Barney admits to being foolish, and perhaps stupid, but he will not be lumped into the ranks of the indecent. Resenting her

implication, fed up with her simpering negativity, he launches into a
tirade that is contrived to shock her back to the reality that there are
still people who are decent, loving, and gentle. And it works.

BARNEY

(*Begins to fume.*) All right! All right, we're all no good. We're all indecent, unfeeling, unloving, rotten human beings. Sick, monstrous,
disgusting people, all of us. You don't know the half of it. You
haven't the slightest idea how filthy and ugly I really am deep inside.
You think you're the first woman I ever had up here? Ha! You want
to hear about Elaine, a woman of Polish persuasion I picked up in my
own restaurant? A drinking, smoking, coughing, married woman
who practically begged me to rip her clothes off. . . . And you know
what happened? *Nothing*, Jeanette. Nothing happened. Because I was
looking for something beautiful, something decent. You want to hear
about Bobbi, a psycho unemployed nightclub singer who had her dog
kidnapped by the Beverly Hills police and sleeps with a Nazi vocal
coach? I sat here with her smoking marijuana and singing popular
songs of the day. . . . And you know what happened? Nothing,
Jeanette. Nothing happened. Because I was looking for something
beautiful something decent. . . . And then I invited you. A woman
who grabbed me in her kitchen last Thursday night and physically
pinned me down on the table. I had mayonnaise stains on my back
when I got home. And when you get here, what do you do? You sit
there taking pills and holding on to your goddamned pocketbook all
day. And again, *nothing* happened, Jeanette. Nothing. Because I was
looking for something beautiful, something decent. Well, I'm
through, dammit. I'm through looking for something beautiful and
decent because *it doesn't exist.* You're right, Jeanette, we're no
damned good, all of us. There are no decent, gentle, loving people
left in the world. (*He advances toward her.*) We're depraved, lustful,
disgusting monsters, all of us. (*He pushes a chair out of the way.*)

But if we're guilty, Jeanette, then let's at least commit the crime. If we're depraved, let's see a little depravity. (*He is moving toward her, she backs away.*) If we're indecent, then let's see a couple of terrific indecencies! *COME HERE, JEANETTE!*

THE GINGERBREAD LADY

Premièred December 13, 1970
at the Plymouth Theatre, New York City

Directed by Robert Moore

CAST

Jimmy Perry	Michael Lombard
Manuel	Alex Colon
Toby Landau	Betsy von Furstenberg
Evy Meara	Maureen Stapleton
Polly Meara	Ayn Ruymen
Lou Tanner	Charles Siebert

The action of the play takes place in a brownstone apartment in the West Seventies of New York City.

Evy Meara, an alcoholic, out-of-work nightclub singer, has returned home after a period of rehabilitation. She is a promiscuous, irresponsible, lonely divorcee who has recently been spurned by Lou Tanner, a younger, impoverished musician. Her best friends are Jimmy Perry, a homosexual, unsuccessful actor, and Toby Landau, a very attractive but decidedly superficial individual. The three are kindred spirits—feckless misfits who lean on each other for support and solace. Then into the mix comes Polly, Evy's teenage daughter.

After three weeks, Evy, still weak and delicately balanced, is feeling the strain of Polly's overweening concern. And, on a fateful evening when Jimmy arrives nearly suicidal due to the fact that he has lost the part in a new play, and Toby arrives shattered because her husband has just announced his plans to divorce, Evy loses herself in a tailspin of drunkenness and engages in insults that alienate those she loves.

After an alcoholic night with Lou Tanner, during which he brutalizes her, Evy returns to be lectured by Toby, who admonishes her for her lifestyle and begs her to release Polly before she is corrupted. And she makes the attempt. But Polly, displaying maturity and grit, refuses to abandon her mother. The play ends on an upbeat note of hope and optimism.

Jimmy. ACT I.

Jimmy is an out-of-work actor and is probably homosexual (probably but not obviously). He is bitchy, caustic and witty. He is also angry and frustrated regarding the the state of his art and career.

In a scene with friend Evy, a recovering alcholic who has just returned from a stay at a local sanitarium, his bitterness and ego surface in a rumination about an upcoming audition.

JIMMY

(*Lost in his own problems.*) I won't get this job tonight. They'll turn me down. I'm auditioning for some nineteen-year-old putz producer who has seventy-five thousand dollars and a drama degree from Oklahoma A & M. . . . First time he walked into the theater he fell off the stage, broke two ribs . . . some chance an intelligent actor has today. . . . Oh God, I want to be a star so bad. Not a little star. I want to be a big star with three agents and two lawyers and a business manager and a press agent and then I'd fire all of them and get new ones because I'm such a big star. And I'd make everyone pay for the twenty-two years I poured into this business. I wouldn't do benefits, I wouldn't give the money to charity. I would become one of the great shitheels of all time. Isn't that a wonderful dream, Evy?

Evy. ACT I.

Daughter Polly has come home and wants to move in with Evy, a recovering alcoholic who has just returned from an extended period of dieting and drying out. But Evy is historically unsuited for motherhood and has serious misgivings about the idea. In this speech, she attempts to dissuade Polly by leveling with her regarding her promiscuous, alcoholic lifestyle.

EVY

You're seventeen years old, it's time you judged me. I just don't want you to get the idea that a hundred and eighty-three pounds of pure alcohol is something called Happy Fat. . . . Many a night I would have thrown myself out that window if I could have squeezed through. . . . I'm not what you'd call an emotionally stable person. You know how many times I was *really* in love since your father and I broke up? I met the only man who ever really meant anything to me about seven maybe eight times. Mr. Right I meet at least twice a week. . . . I sure know true love when I see it. It's wherever I happen to look.

Intervening speech. Polly: You don't have to tell me any of this.

EVY (*cont'd.*)

I *do*, dammit. . . . I want you to know everything, Polly, before you make up your mind. I lived here with that guitar player for eight of the happiest months of my life. Well, why not? He was handsome, funny, ten years younger than me, what more could a woman want? . . . He sat in that chair all day working and writing and I fed him and clothed him and loved him for eight incredible months. . . . And then that dirty bastard—I'm sorry, I'm going to try not to do that anymore.

Intervening speech. Polly: Good.

EVY (*cont'd.*)

No, the hell with it. That dirty bastard. He walked out on me in the middle of the night for an eighteen-year-old Indian hippie. "Princess-Screw-the-Other-Woman." . . . Wait'll she gets old and starts looking like the face on the nickel. And he doesn't have a penny, not a cent. Well, her moccasins'll wear out, we'll see how long that affair lasts.

. . . But I sat at that window for six weeks waiting and hoping while I ran through two liquor stores in this neighborhood alone. . . . Finally Toby came in one day and found me face down in the bathtub. . . . I woke up in a sanitarium in Long Island, and the rest isn't very interesting unless you like stories about human torture. . . . But I went through it and I'm here. And I figure, pussycat, that I have only one more chance at this human being business . . . and if I blow it this time, they'll probably bury me in some distillery in Kentucky. . . . And if this is the kind of person you'd like to live with, God has cursed me with one of the all-time great schumucks for a daughter.

Toby: ACT II.

Evy has arranged a fortieth birthday celebration for her friend Toby. When Toby arrives alone, she reveals that husband Martin is not coming because he has just asked for a divorce on grounds of sexual incompatibility. Toby, an extremely vain, attractive woman, one who has always been sexually desirable, is devastated.

TOBY

(*Takes a deep breath.*) Martin—has grown accustomed to my face. (*She is visibly wounded but is trying hard not to show the hurt.*) . . . Accustomed to my touch, accustomed to my voice . . . and I think he's a little bored with my hair. (*Looks at them, forces a smile, sips a little wine.*) . . . He's devoted to me. . . . He is respectful of me. . . . He is indebted to me . . . but he's having a lot of trouble sleeping with me. For some inexplicable reason . . . "inexplicable" is his word . . . he has had no desire to make sexual advances towards me. . . . He makes them, but there's no desire. . . . It's as though someone were in back of him "pushing." . . . He is not tired . . . he is not overworked . . . he is not distracted. . . . He is simply— "turned off." That's *my* word.

Intervening speech. Jimmy: (*About to say something helpful.*) Toby, for God's sake—

TOBY (*cont'd.*)

Did you know . . . that in 1950 I was voted the prettiest girl at the University of Michigan? . . . An All-American halfback was willing to give up a trip to the Rose Bowl for one night of my favors. . . . in 1951 I switched schools and was voted the prettiest girl at the University of Southern California. . . . I received on the average of fifteen sexual proposals a week . . . at least two from the faculty. . . .

Intervening speech. Evy: All right, Toby. . . .

TOBY (*cont'd.*)

When I was sixteen I was offered a seven-year contract by R.K.O. Pictures. They knew I couldn't act, they didn't even care. They said they way I looked, it wasn't important. . . . When I was seventeen years old, a married psychiatrist in Los Angeles drove his car into a tree because I wouldn't answer his phone calls. You can read all of this in my diaries, I still have them.

Intervening speech. Evy: Toby, please stop.

TOBY (*cont'd.*)

When I was nineteen I had an affair with a boy who was the son of the largest book publisher in the world. . . . When I was twenty, I had an affair *with* the largest book publisher in the world. . . . The son threatened to kill the father but by then I was having an affair with the youngest symphony conductor in the world.

Intervening speech. Evy: Jimmy, for God's sake, will you say something to her?

TOBY *(cont'd.)*

(Accelerating.) When I was twenty-three, I *slept* with a member of the British Royal Household. I slept with him. In the British Royal House. . . . There is a senator living in Washington, D.C., today, who will vote any way I want him to vote by spending just one morning in Washington, D.C. . . . I have had more men, men in politics, in the arts, in the sciences, more of the most influential men in the world, in love with me, desirous of me, *hungry* for me, than any woman I ever met in my entire life . . . and that son-of-a-bitch, four-hundred-dollar-a-week television salesman tells me *he isn't interested?. . . Then let him get out, I don't need him! (And she begins to sob uncontrollably.)* Evy . . . Evy . . . !

Toby. ACT II.

Hurt and angered by being sexually unattractive to her husband, Toby continues her outpouring. Couched in her revelations is the sad fact that she is unable to see that her superficiality is at the core of her marital problem.

TOBY

(She sips a little more of her champagne.) I'm not a stupid woman, I know that. I've traveled a lot, I'm well-read, well-educated, I went to two universities. . . . I have had marvelous, intellectual conversations with some of the most brilliant men in the world. . . but the things that men admire most in a woman are her femininity and her beauty. . . . That's the truth, Evy, I know it is. *(To Jimmy.)* Isn't that the first thing you men look for in a woman, Jimmy?

Intervening speech. Jimmy: *(Hesitates.)* . . . Yes, I suppose it is.

TOBY (*cont'd.*)

(*Back to Evy.*) . . . I know I'm vain, Evy, I never pretended I'm not. I devote my whole day to myself, to my face, to my body. . . . I sleep all morning so my eyes won't be red. . . . I bathe twice a day in soft water, I buy the world's most expensive creams, I have a Japanese man who lives in White Plains come down twice a week just to do my feet. Did you know that, Evy? (*Evy nods. Toby turns to Jimmy.*) Did you?

Intervening speech. Jimmy: I didn't know he was Japanese.

TOBY (*cont'd.*)

I swear. He says I have the feet of an Oriental woman. . . . Can you imagine, Evy. Born in Grand Rapids, Michigan, with the feet of an Oriental woman. . . . But I've never done it for me. None of it. . . . It's what Martin wanted when he came into his house at night, what all men want. . . . Femininity and beauty. . . . But, Evy—if it no longer interests Martin . . . then I assure you . . . somewhere soon, someplace, someone else will be very . . . very . . . very . . . interested! (*Her voice has trailed off almost becoming inaudible at the end. There is a long, desperate silence in the room.*)

Evy. ACT II.

The events of the evening have taken their toll on Evy, a recovering alcoholic just three weeks out of the sanitarium. First her daughter chastises her for arriving home late for dinner and then displays ridiculous, overprotective tendencies. Secondly, Jimmy, her long-time actor friend, arrives despondent and shattered because he has been dropped from a play just three days before opening. Then in a crowning touch, her best friend, Toby, arrives for her fortieth birthday party with the news that her husband is filing for divorce. Evy, still in a state of fragile vulnerability, is sent into an emotional tail-spin. She lapses into a state of drunken sarcasm, alienating those she loves. Toby and Jimmy flee, and daughter Polly retreats to her bedroom with the exit lines: "I'm sorry . . . I'm just plain sorry."

At the end of this speech, which closes Act Two, Evy, alone, contrite and inebriated, calls Lou Tanner, an ex-lover who left her for a younger woman.

EVY

(*Loudly.*) Sorry for what? For me? Well, don't be sorry for me because I don't need your Goddamned teenage pity. . . . I'm terrific, baby, haven't you noticed? Cost me 27 hundred bucks and I'm skinny and terrific and I can have any dirty old man in the neighborhood. . . . (*Suddenly softening.*) Oh, Jesus, Polly, I'm sorry. . . . (*She crosses to the bedroom door.*) Polly, don't be mad. . . . Come on out, we'll have our own private party. . . . Look! Look, I'm gonna put on some music. (*She crosses to record player.*) I've just had a request to play one of my old numbers. (*Takes out her album.*) Come listen to Mother sing when she was a big star, darling. (*She puts record on machine.*) Well not exactly a big star. . . . But I once had a sandwich named after me at the Stage Delicatessen. . . . (*The MUSIC STARTS. . . . We hear Evy singing. . . . She stands there listening, drinking from her wine glass.*) . . . That's not bad, is it? . . . It's not bad. . . . It's not *thrilling* but it's not bad. . . . (*She sings along, looks around.*) This is about the same size audiences I used to get. . . . (*She crosses to bedroom door.*) Polly, please come out. . . . I don't want to listen to me all by myself. . . . Polly? (*No answer. Looks at the PHONE.*) I am *not* going to listen all by myself. . . . (*Crosses to PHONE. . . . takes a deep breath and dials. Into PHONE:*) Hello? Lou? . . . You alone? . . . Guess who wants to come over to your place?

Toby. ACT III.

It is morning and Toby is in the apartment when Evy returns from an all-niter with former lover Lou Tanner. She is hung over, disheveled, and sporting a shiner. During a heated confrontation between them, Toby takes Evy to task for her drunkenness and pleads with her not to allow Polly to become another casualty of her irresponsible lifestyle.

TOBY

You're not twenty-two, you're forty-three. And you're an alcoholic with no sense of morality or responsibility. You've never had a lasting relationship with anyone who wasn't as weak or as helpless as yourself. So you have friends like Jimmy and me. Misfits who can't do any more than pick up your discarded clothes and empty glasses. We all hold each other up because none of us has the strength to do it alone. And lovers like Lou Tanner whose only talent is to beat your bloody face in and leave you when something better comes along. I know what I am, Evy. I don't like it and I never have. So I cover the outside with Helena Rubenstein. I use little makeup jars, you use quart bottles. . . . And poor Jimmy uses a little of both. . . . Some terrific people. . . . But by some strange miracle, in there—(*Indicating bedroom.*)—is a girl who is crazy in love with you because she's too young to know any better. . . . But keep it up, Evy, and she'll get to know better before you can say Jack Daniels. . . . The way I see it, you've got two choices: Either get a book on how to be a mature, responsible person . . . or get her out of here before you destroy her chance to become one. . . . There's your honesty and truth, Evy. . . . It's a perfect fit. How do you like it?

THE PRISONER of SECOND AVENUE
(L)

Premièred November 11, 1971
at the Eugene O'Neill Theatre, New York City.

CAST

Mel Edison	Peter Falk
Edna Edison	Lee Grant
Harry Edison	Vincent Gardenia
Pearl	Florence Stanley
Jessie	Tresa Hughes
Pauline	Dena Dietrich

The action of the play takes place in the Edison's 14th floor apartment on New York's East Side.

The pressures of urban life are getting to Mel Edison, an account executive with a New York advertising agency. His apartment is noisy and poorly maintained, crime is rampant, air and noise pollution is unbearable, the city is filthy, and after twenty-two years he is afraid of losing his job. He is tense, anxious, and suffering from insomnia. Then his apartment is literally cleaned out by thieves. They even take the Valium! To further complicate matters, his worst fears are then realized when he is fired. As a final blow to his dignity, he is doused with water by his upstairs neighbor, an act that solidifies his negative feelings regarding the sad state of humankind. Like a loyal soldier, wife Edna takes a job as a secretary to tide them over until Mel finds work. But his job-hunting efforts prove futile and he becomes a depressed recluse, climbing the walls of his apartment. Humiliated at living off of Edna's income, his feeling of self-worth shattered, Mel lapses into a state of deep depression, extreme paranoia, and a burning need to retaliate against the water-dumper upstairs—at the first snowfall he plans to bury the son of a bitch as he enters the building below. He suffers a breakdown, which requires sedation and psychiatric care.

Mel's older brother, Harry, and his two sisters, in an apparent act of family caring, come to offer help. But the underlying reality of costs results in bickering, discord, and disagreement, and Edna spurns them for their lack of true compassion.

After several weeks of therapy, Mel, greatly improved, realizes that Edna is showing symptoms he had experienced as a result of workplace pressures. And, when she informs him that she, too, is out of work because of business failure, he is positive, contained, and supportive, further testimony to the fact that he is mentally stable. When brother Harry arrives with a no-strings-attached check for twenty-five thousand dollars, Mel is touched but rejects his offer. Mel, during a touching exchange, learns that Harry, a successful businessman, has never felt loved, and that he has always envied Mel as family favorite.

At play's end, heavy snow begins to fall on the city. Mel goes to a closet and removes a snow shovel he has reserved for the purpose of getting revenge on the son of a bitch above. He and Edna represent a picture of solidarity, committed to braving whatever the future holds.

Mel. ACT I. Scene ii.

Unemployed, with financial obligations, anxious about the future, Mel rails against the superficial trappings that clutter our lives and complicate living.

MEL

I don't mean out of here. Out of obligations. Out of things we don't need that are choking us. I'm gonna quit the gym. I don't need a gym for two hundred and fifty dollars a year. I'll run around the bedroom, it's the only way to keep warm in there anyway . . . And we don't need the Modern Museum of Art. We can watch *Duck Soup* on television. (*Picks up magazines.*) And these Goddamn magazines. I don't want *Time*, *Life* or *Newsweek* anymore, you understand. I'm not going to spend my last few dollars to find out that unemployment went up this year. (*He throws them into wastebasket.*)

Intervening speech. Edna: We don't need *any* of them. We never did, Mel.

MEL (*cont'd.*)

(*Looking around, throwing more junk in basket.*) The garbage! The garbage that we buy every year. Useless, meaningless garbage that fills up the house until you throw it out there and it becomes garbage again and *stinks* up the house. For what? For *what*, Edna?

Intervening speech. Edna: I don't know, Mel.

MEL (*cont'd.*)

Two dollars worth of food that comes in three dollars worth of wrapping. Telephone calls to find out what time it is because you're too lazy to look at a clock . . . The food we never ate, the books we never read, the records we never played. (*He picks up a little thing off the bar.*) Look at this! Eight and a half dollars for a musical whiskey pourer. *Eight and a half dollars!* God forbid we should get a little bored while we're pouring our whiskey! Toys! Toys, novelties, gimmicks, trivia, garbage, crap, HORSESHIT! (*He hurls the basket to floor.*)

Intervening speech. Edna: No more. We'll never buy another thing, Mel. I promise. I promise.

MEL (*cont'd.*)

(*He is seething with anger.*) Twenty-two years I gave them. What did I give them twenty-two years of my life for? A musical whiskey pourer? It's my *life* that's being poured down the drain. Where's the music? Where's a cute little tune? They kick you out after twenty-two years, they ought to have a Goddamned brass band.

Edna. ACT I. Scene ii.

Mel has worked himself into a state of anxiety to the point of experiencing chest pains. His profane ranting has raised a complaint from his neighbor above. When he rushes to his balcony to do verbal battle, the neighbor douses him with water. Sick with anxiety, disillusioned that a human being could be so callous as to dump water on another, he lapses into a state of quiet sobbing. In this speech closing Act One, Edna does her best to comfort him.

EDNA

(*Wiping him.*) Never. You're too good, Mel, too decent . . . You would never do that . . . It's going to be all right, Mel, I promise . . . You'll get another job, you'll see . . . And we'll move away from here. Someplace far away . . . You know what we could do? You're so good with kids, you love being with them, we could start a summer camp . . . You would be the head of the camp and I would do the cooking and the girls can be the riding instructors and the swimming instructors. You would like that, wouldn't you, Mel? We'll just have to save some money, that's all. And if you don't get another job right away, I can always be a secretary again. I can work, I'm strong, Mel . . . But you mustn't get sick. You mustn't get sick and die because I don't want to live in this world without you . . . I don't like it here! . . . I don't want you to leave me alone here . . . We'll show them, Mel . . . We'll show them all . . .

Edna. ACT II. Scene i.

Six weeks later. Edna has taken a job as secretary in order to bolster finances until Mel finds work. She is overworked and harried, but she lovingly returns home every day to prepare Mel's lunch. Here, in a monologue that opens Scene One, she relates her weariness. Mel, despondent, depressed by the turn of events, is unresponsive.

EDNA

Mel? . . . Mel, I'm home. (*She closes the door and crosses to the living room, turns off radio, then into kitchen.*) You must be starved. I'll have your lunch in a second . . . (*Takes things out of package.*) I couldn't get out of the office until a quarter to one and then I had to wait fifteen minutes for a bus . . . God, the traffic on Third Avenue during lunch hour . . . I got a cheese soufflé in Schrafft's, is that all right? I just don't have time to fix anything today, Mr. Cooperman wants me back before two o'clock, we're suddenly swamped with work this week . . . He asked if I would come in on Saturdays from now until Christmas but I told him I didn't think I could . . . (*She is crossing to the kitchen and is getting out pots.*) I mean we could use the extra money but I don't think I want to spend Saturdays in that office too. We see each other little enough now as it is . . . Come in and talk to me while I'm cooking, Mel, I've only got about thirty-five minutes today . . . (*Edna has put the casserole on the stove and is now crossing into kitchen, setting up two places with dishes and silverware.*) . . . My feet are absolutely killing me. I don't know why they gave me a desk because I haven't had a chance to sit at it in a month . . . Hi, Love. I bought you Sports Illustrated . . . Mr. Cooperman told me there's a terriffic story in there about the Knicks, he thought you might be interested in it . . . (*Mel tosses the magazine aside with some contempt . . .*) . . . You just can't move up Third Avenue because there's one of those protest parades up Fifth Avenue, or down Fifth Avenue, whichever way they protest . . . Fifteen thousand women screaming "Save the Environment" and they're all wearing leopard coats . . . God, the hypocrisy . . . Come on, sit down, I've got some tomato juice first . . . (*She pours tomato juice into two glasses. Mel listlessly moves to table and sits.*) . . . Isn't that terrible about the Commissioner of Police? . . . I mean *kidnapping* the New York Commissioner of Police? . . . Isn't that insane? I mean if the cops can't find him, they can't find anybody . . . (*She sits, picks up her glass of tomato juice and sips.*) . . . Oh, God, that's good. That's the first food I've had since eight o'clock this morning. We're so busy there we don't even have time for a coffee break . . . He's going to ask me to work nights, I know it, and I just don't know what to say to him . . . I mean he's been so nice to me, he buys me sandwiches two or three times a week, not that I don't deserve it, the way I've been working this past month, but I just don't want to spend any nights down there because I don't even have the strength to talk when I get home anymore . . . I don't know where I'm getting the energy, I must have been saving it up for the past twenty-two years . . . (*She sips again.*) . . . I've got to stop talking because I'm all wound up and I'll never stop . . . How are you, darling? You feeling all right? (*Mel sits, staring into his tomato juice.*) . . . Mel? You all right?

Mel. ACT II. Scene i.

Mel, unable to find work, has lapsed into a state of deep depression and paranoid, delusional behavior. Blaming the entire human race for an insidious "plot" against him, he expresses his humiliation for being unemployed and his plans of sweet revenge against the tenant above who doused him with water.

MEL

You don't know the first thing I'm talking about . . . You don't know what it is to be in my place . . . You're never stood on line for two hours waiting for an unemployment check with a shirt and tie, trying to look like you don't need the money . . . And some fat old dame behind the counter screaming out so everyone can hear, *"Did you look for a job this week?"* . . . "Yes, I looked for a job" . . . *"Did you turn down any work this week?"* . . . "What the hell am I doing here if I turned down work this week?" . . . You never walked into your own building and have a ninety-one-year-old doorman with no teeth, asthma and beer on his breath giggle at you because *he's* working . . . You've never been on your own terrace and gotten hit with a bucket of ice cold water . . . I haven't forgotten that son of a bitch! (*He goes to terrace, but not out on it, and yells up.*) . . . I haven't forgotten you, you son of a bitch!

Intervening speech. Edna: Mel, don't start in again. Please don't start in again.

MEL (*cont'd.*)

I'm waiting for him. I'm just waiting for him. He's up there now but one day he's gonna be down there and I'm gonna be up here and then we'll see. One cold, snowy day some son of a bitch in this building is gonna be buried under three feet of snow. They won't find him until spring. (*Yells up again.*) They won't find you until the spring, you son-of-a-bitch!

Harry. ACT II. Scene ii.

Mel has had a nervous collapse and is undergoing psychiatric treat-
ment. Concerned for his mental well-being and shaky financial situa-
tion, Mel's older brother, Harry, and sisters, Jessie and Pearl, have
come to offer assistance. While Edna is in the bedroom speaking with
Mel's doctor on the phone, the trio engages in petty criticism and
bickering that has little to do with the central issue of Mel's problem.
Finally, Harry, the primary spokesman for the group, offers a solu-
tion. But during his speech proposing assistance, Harry can't refrain
from passing judgment.

HARRY

Fact number three, besides a nervous breakdown and not having a job, the man is practically penniless . . . I don't want to pass any comments on how a man and a woman mishandled their money for twenty-seven years, it's none of my business how a man squandered a life's savings on bad investments for which he never asked my ad-vice once, the kind of advice which has given me solvency, security and a beautiful summer place in the country, thank God, *I'll* never have a nervous breakdown . . . none of that is my business. My business is what we are going to do for Mel? How much are we go-ing to give? Somebody make a suggestion. (*The silence is deafening.*
No one speaks. No one even looks at each other. There is a lot of
coffee drinking, but no one offers of how much they are going to give
. . . After an hour of silence, Harry speaks again.) . . . Well?

Intervening speech. Pearl: You're a businessman, Harry. You make a suggestion. You tell us how much we should all give.

HARRY (*cont'd.*)

(*Thinks a moment.*) . . . Let me have some coffee. (*Pearl pours him a cup of coffee.*) So let's face the facts . . . The man needs help. Who else can he turn to but us? This is my suggestion . . . We make Mel a loan. We all chip in X number of dollars a week, and then when he gets back on his feet, when he gets straightened out, gets a job again, then he can pay us all back. That's my suggestion. What do you all think?

Mel. ACT II. Scene iii.

Mel, regaining his stability, has decided to give up therapy.

MEL

. . . I'm not going back. I'm not going back to that doctor. He's a quack. He sits there cleaning his pipe, playing with his watch fob and doesn't know what the hell he's talking about. The man is a quack. If I'm getting better, I'm doing it myself . . . I'm working my *own* problems out. That man sits there playing with a pipe scooper watching *me* get better for forty dollars an hour . . . I got mirrors in the house, I can watch myself get better. I could lay there for fifty minutes, if I don't say a word, he won't say a word. Would it kill him (*During this, he has been crossing to closet, putting paint box, easel, and canvas away.*) to ask me a question? "What's wrong, Mr. Edison? What are you thinking about?" . . . Not him. If I don't bring it up, he don't ask. I'm curing myself, I'm telling you. I see how you look when you come home every night. Killing yourself, breaking your back and for what? To give forty dollars an hour to a pipe cleaner? I can't take it anymore, Edna. I can't see you turning yourself into an old woman, just for me. What's the point in it? As soon as I'm all right again, I'll be too young for you.

THE SUNSHINE BOYS
(V L)

Premièred on December 20, 1972
at the Broadhurst Theatre, New York City

Directed by Alan Arkin

CAST

Willie Clark	Jack Albertson
Ben Silverman	Lewis J. Stadlen
Al Lewis	Sam Levene
Patient	Joe Young
Eddie	John Batiste
Nurse	Lee Meredith
Registered Nurse	Minnie Gentry

The action of the play takes place in an apartment-hotel on upper Broadway.

Willie Clark, one half of the old comedy team Lewis and Clark, is a cantankerous old vaudevillian living alone in a dilapidated New York hotel. His nephew/agent, Ben, looks after him and unsuccessfully attempts to find work for his acerbic, doddering uncle, who still has designs on show business. Al Lewis, a mild-mannered sort, is now retired and lives with his daughter and son-in-law in New Jersey.

Willie, embittered because Al broke up their act to become a stock broker, has not spoken to him for eleven years.

After much cajoling, Ben is successful in getting the old partners to recreate their famous comedy sketch for CBS television. During a dress rehearsal at the CBS, old wounds are opened, an argument ensues, and Al walks off the set. Willie, who has worked himself into a lather, collapses with a heart attack.

Recuperating in his hotel room, Willie is still the caustic old show-biz warrior. But Ben tells him that his active entertainment days are over and convinces him to move into the Actors Home in New Brunswick. He also tells him that Al Lewis is in the lobby, is greatly concerned, and wants to pay his respects. Grudgingly, Willie agrees to receive him.

Willie is imperious and insulting and there is nearly another split, but under the acid veneer, it's apparent that there's warmth for his old partner. Willie tells Al affectionately that he is a pain in the ass, but a funny man, and, in a ironic twist, Al informs Willie that he is going to be moving into the Actors Home in New Brunswick. The play ends with the old troupers recalling the halcyon days of vaudeville.

Willie. ACT I.

Willie, one half of the comedy team Lewis and Clark, has not seen or spoken to Al Lewis for eleven years. When Ben, Willie's agent-nephew pleads with him to recreate their famous Doctor sketch for CBS, he is intractable. Here he tells the reason for his animosity toward his old partner.

WILLIE

What about a "classic"! A *classic*! . . . A *dead* person watching that sketch would laugh . . . We did it maybe eight thousand times, it never missed . . . *That* night it missed . . . Something was wrong with him, he was rushing, his timing was off, his mind was someplace else . . . I thought he was sick . . . still we got terrific applause . . . Five times Ed Sullivan said, "How about that"? . . . We got back into the dressing room, he took off his make-up, put on his clothes and said to me, "Willie, if it's all the same to you, I'm retiring." . . . I said, "What do you mean, retiring? It's not even nine o'clock. Let's have something to eat." . . . He said, "I'm not retiring for the night. I'm retiring for what's left of my life" . . . And he puts on his hat, walked out of the theater, becomes a stock broker and I'm left with an act where I ask questions and there's no on there to answer . . . Never saw the man again to this day . . . Oh, he called me, I wouldn't answer . . . He wrote me, I tore it up . . . He sent me telegrams, they're probably still under the door.

THE GOOD DOCTOR

Premièred November 27, 1973
at the Eugene O'Neill Theatre, New York City

Directed by A. J. Antoon

CAST

"The Writer"   Christopher Plummer

"The Sneeze"   Christopher Plummer,
　　　　　Rene Auberjonois, Marsha Mason,
　　　　　Barnard Hughes, Frances Sternhagen

"The Governess" Frances Sternhagen, Marsha Mason

"Surgery"   Christopher Plummer, Barnard
　　　　　Hughes

"Too Late for Happiness" Barnard Hugues, Frances
　　　　　Sternhagen

"The Seduction" Christopher Plummer, Rene
　　　　　Auberjonois, Marsha Mason

"The Drowned Man" Christopher Plummer, Rene
　　　　　Auberjonois, Barnard Hughes

"The Audition"   Christopher Plummer,
　　　　　Marsha Mason

"The Defenseless Creature"   Christopher Plummer,
　　　　　Rene Auberjonois, Marsha Mason

"The Quiet War" Christopher Plummer

The *Good Doctor* is twelve vignettes sprung from the creative imagination of a Writer/Narrator. Each, with ironic humor, is an incisive comment on social interaction and the human condition. Homage to Anton Chekhov is obvious

"The Writer."

Narrator. ACT I. Scene i.

This monologue introduces the piece. The Russian aspects, plus language taken from Trigorin's speech in The Seagull, *establish the Chekovian mode for the sketches that follow.*

NARRATOR

. . . It's quite all right, you're not disturbing me. . . . I would much rather talk than work, yet here I am, day after day haunted by one thought, I must write, I must write, I must write. . . . This is my study, the room in which I write my stories. I built it myself, actually . . . cut the timber and fitted the logs. . . . Made an awful mess of it. . . . I do my writing here at the side of the room because the roof leaks directly over my desk. . . . I'd move the desk but it covers a hole I left in the floor. . . . And the floor was built on the side of the hill so in heavy rains, the room tends to slide downhill. . . . Many's the day I have stood in this cabin and passed my neighbors standing in the road. . . . Still, I'm happy here. . . . Although I don't get enough visitors to suit me. . . . People tend to shy away from writers. . . . They assume we're always busy thinking, not true. . . . Even my dear sweet Mother doesn't like to disturb me so she always tiptoes up here and leaves my food outside the door. . . . I haven't had a hot meal in years. . . . But I've done a good deal of writing in here. . . . Perhaps too much. . . . I look out the window and think that life is passing me at a furious rate. So, I ask myself the question . . . what force is it that compels me to write so incessantly, day after day, page after page, story after story. . . . And the answer is quite simple. . . . I have no choice. . . . I am a writer. . . . Sometimes I think I may be mad. . . . Oh, I'm quite harmless. . . . But I do admit to fits of wandering. . . . I'm engaged in conversations where I hear nothing and see only the silent movement of lips and answer a meaningless, "yes, yes, of course" and all the time I'm thinking, "He'll make a wonderful character for a story, this one." . . . Still, while I'm writing I enjoy it. And I like reading the proofs, but . . . as soon as it appears in print, I can't bear it. I see that it's all wrong, a mistake, that it ought never to have been written, and I am miserable. . . . Then the public reads it: "Yes, charming, clever. . . . Charming but a far cry from Tolstoy" . . . or "A fine thing, but Turgenev's 'Fathers and Sons' is better." . . . And so it will be to my dying day. . . . Charming and clever, charming and clever, nothing more . . . and when I die my friends will walk by my grave and say, "here lies so and so, a good writer, but Turgenev was better." . . . It's funny, but before you came in, I was thinking to myself, perhaps I should give it up one day. . . . What would I do instead? . . . Well, I've never freely admitted this before, but to you here in the theater tonight, I would like to tell you what I would most like to do with my life. . . . Ever since I was a small child, I always . . . I always . . . —Excuse me a moment.—Just making a note. . . . And idea just occurred to me. A subject for a short story. . . . Hmm, yes, yes. . . . It was my mentioning the theater that sparked me. . . . What were we talking about a moment ago. . . . No matter. My thoughts are consumed with this new story. . . . See if this appeals to you. . . . It starts in a theater. [*Cue 1.*] . . . It starts on the opening night of the new season. [*Cue 2.*] . . . It starts [*Cue 3.*] with the arrival of all those dear and devoted patrons of the arts who wave and greet each other in the Grand Salon, commenting on how this one looks and how that one is dressed—scarcely knowing what play they are about to see that evening. [*Cue 3 out.*] . . . With the exception of one man . . . Ivan Ilyitch Cherdyakov! [*Cue 4.*] (*The Theater Set appears.*)

"Surgery."

Narrator. ACT I.

The previous sketch "The Governess" showed how class distinction during the days of the czars reduced the lower classes to fearful chattel. In this preamble to the Narrator/Writer's next fiction, he offers an alternative ending to the previous scene and sets up the next—a tragicomic skit in which a dental patient is the unwitting victim of a good doctor's inexperienced, heavy-handed assistant.

NARRATOR

Wait! [*Cue 13 out.*] For those again who are offended by life's cruelty, there is an alternate ending . . . Julia was so enraged by such cruel and unjust treatment—that she quit her job on the spot and went back to her poor parents—where she inherited five million rubles . . . It is my intention someday to write a book of 37 short stories—all with that same ending. I do love it so. . . . You know that it has been said that Man is the only living creature that is capable of laughter and it is that faculty that separates us from the lower forms of life. . . . Yet, one must wonder about this theory when we examine some of the objects of our laughter. . . . For example, Pain. . . . Pain, needless to say, is no laughing matter . . . unless of course, it's someone else who is doing the suffering. . . . Why the sight of a man in the throes of excruciating agony from an abscessed tooth that has enlarged his jaw to the size of an orange is funny, I couldn't say. . . . It is *not* funny. . . . Not in the least. But in the village of Astemko, [*Cue 14.*] where they have very little access to entertainment, a man with a toothache can tickle their ribs for weeks. . . . Certainly, Sergie Vonmiglasov, the sexton, saw nothing humorous about it. . . . (*The lights come up on the Surgery Room. . . . There is a chair on one side and on the other is a table with various medical instruments. . . .*

Enter the Sexton, Vonmiglasov. . . . He is a large, heavy-set man wearing a cassock and a wide belt. He is a priest in the Russian Church. A scarf is wrapped around his face and his jaw is enlarged. He crosses the stage and moans in pain.) Yet, as he passed through the village on his way to the hospital, his moans and groans won him more chuckles than sympathetic remarks. Wouldn't they find it even more amusing to know that the good doctor who normally performed the extractions of angry teeth was away at the wedding of his daughter, and the duty fell to his new assistant, Kuryatin, an eager medical student, if, alas poor sexton, an inexperienced one.

"The Seduction."

Peter. ACT I. Scene vi.

Peter Semyonych is the greatest seducer of women, especially married women. In this speech he tells how, by artfully communicating to the wife through her husband, he establishes his desirability.

PETER

. . . If I may say so myself, I am the greatest seducer of other men's wives that I've ever met. . . . I say this not boastfully, but as a matter of record. The staggering figures speak for themselves. . . . For those men interested in playing this highly satisfying but often dangerous game, I urge you to take out pen and paper and take notes. . . . I am going to explain my methods. . . . In defense, married women may do likewise but it will do them little good if they happen to be the chosen victim. . . . My method has never failed. . . . Now then, there are three vital characteristics needed. . . . They are, patience, more patience, and still more patience. . . . Those who do not have the strength to wait and persist, I urge you to take up bicycling. . . . rowing, perhaps. . . . Seducing isn't for you. . . . Now then, in order to seduce a man's wife, you must, I repeat *must*, keep as far away from her as possible. . . . Pay her practically no attention at all. . . . Ignore her if you must. . . . We will get to her—through the *husband.* [*Cue 2.*] . . . (*He looks at his watch, then off into the wings.*) You are about to witness a practical demonstration, for as it happens I am madly and deeply in love this week. . . . My heart pounds with excitement knowing that she will pass through this garden in a few moments with her husband. Every fiber of my being tells me to throw my arms around her and embrace her with all the passion in my heart. . . . But observe how a master works . . . I shall be cool almost to the point of freezing. . . . My heart of hearts and spouse, approaches. [*Cue 2 out.*] (*He turns the other way as the Husband and his lovely, younger Bride approach taking an afternoon stroll in the park. She carries an umbrella to shade the afternoon sun.*)

PETER. ACT I. Scene vi.

During an encounter with friend Nikolaich and his younger, pretty wife Irena, Peter, through his conversation with her husband, has laid the groundwork for her seduction.

PETER

(*Doffs his hat.*) Madame! (*Turns to audience.*) . . . Beautifully done, don't you think? . . . I'm sometimes awed by the work of a true professional. . . . Did you notice our eyes barely met, we exchanged hardly a word and yet how much she knows of me already. A) I am a popular bachelor, B) a man in love (always titillating to romantic women), C) a gifted sportsman (a nice contrast to her sedentary husband) and D) and this is most important, a dangerous man with the ladies. . . . Quite frankly, at this point she is disgusted by me . . . A) because I'm a braggart and a scoundrel, B) because I am shamelessly frank as to my intentions and C) because she thinks she's not the one

I'm interested in. . . . Forgive me if I'm slightly overcome by my own deviousness. . . . By the way, are you getting this all down? It gets tricky from here on in. . . . Now then, next step, hypnosis . . . not hypnosis with your eyes, but with the poison of your tongue much like a venomous snake moving in for the kill . . . and what's more, the best channel is the husband himself. . . . Witness, as I "accidentally" run into him one day at the club. . . . (*He crosses to the "Club." . . . The Husband is sitting reading a newspaper. . . . Peter takes up a newspaper and sits next to him. The husband looks up and notices him.*)

Wife. ACT I. Scene vi.

Through her husband, Peter has deftly passed information to Irena that has made him irrestible to her. Learning that he will be in the park, she rushes to him passionately, offering herself completely. Peter has once again successfuly seduced a married woman. But irony intervenes when Irena tells him that their affair will destroy her marriage for all time, and offers him a choice which results in him turning his attentions from married to single women—and eventually taking a wife.

WIFE

No! . . . Not a word! . . . Not a sound! . . . Please! . . . I couldn't bear it. . . . Not until you've heard what's in my heart. (*She takes a moment to compose herself.*) . . . For weeks now I've been in torment. . . . You've used my husband a clever and devious device to arouse my passions . . . which I freely admit, have been lying dormant these past seven years. . . . Whether you are sincere or not, you have awakened in me desires and longings I never dreamt were possible. . . . You appeal to my vanity and I succumb. You bestir my thoughts of untold pleasures and I weaken. You attack my every vulnerability and I surrender. I am here, Peter Semyonych, if you want me. (*He starts to reach for her but she holds up her hand for him to stop.*) But let me add this. I love my husband dearly. He is not a passionate man, nor even re-motely romantic. Our life together reaches neither the heights of ecstasy nor the depths of anguish. We have an *even* marriage. Moderate and comfortable . . . and in accepting this condition and the full measure of his devoted love, I have been happy. . . . I come to you now knowing that once you take me in your arms, my marriage and my life With Nicky will be destroyed for all time. . . . I am too weak and too selfish to make the choice . . . I rely on your strength of character. . . . The option is yours, my dear Peter. Whichever one you chose will make me both miserable and eternally grateful. . . . I beg of you not to use me as an amusement . . . although even with that knowledge, I would not refuse you. I am yours to do as you will, Peter Semyonych. . . . If you want me, open your arms now and I will come to you. . . . If you love me, turn your back and I will leave, and never see or speak to you again. . . . The choice, my dearest, sweetest love of my life is yours . . . I await your decision. (*Peter looks at her, then turns his head and looks full face at the audience. . . . He wants some advice but none is coming. . . . He turns back to the Wife. . . . He starts to raise his arms for her but they will not budge. It is as though they weighed ten tons each. . . . He struggles again with no results. He makes one final effort and then quickly changes his mind and turns his back on her.*) God bless you, Peter Semyonych . . . I wish life brings you the happiness you have just brought to me. (*She turns and runs off U. L.*)

"The Audition."

Girl. ACT II. Scene ii.

An inexperienced young girl has come from Odessa to audition for Chekhov. He attempts to dissuade her due to her lack of professionalism, but she convinces him to allow her to read a speech from his play The Three Sisters. *Her rendition is surprisingly good, resulting in her being recalled by Chekhov.*

GIRL

And Masha says, "Oh, listen to that music. They are leaving us. One has gone for good. Forever. We are left alone to begin our life over again. . . . We must live . . . we must live . . . " And Irina says, " . . . A time will come when everyone will know what all this is for . . . (*She is reading with more feeling and compassion than we expected.*) . . . why there is all this suffering, and there will be no mysteries, but meanwhile we must live . . . we must work, only work. . . . Tomorrow I shall go alone, and I shall teach in the school, and give my whole life to those who need it. . . . Now it is autumn, soon winter will come and cover everything with snow, and I shall go on working, working . . . " Shall I finish?

Intervening speech. Voice: (*Softly.*) Please.

GIRL (*cont'd.*)

And Olga says, " . . . The music plays so gaily, so valiantly, one wants to live. Oh, my God. Time will pass, and we shall be gone forever . . . we'll be forgotten. Our faces will be forgotten, our voices, and how many there were of us, but our sufferings will turn into joy for those who live after us, happiness and peace will come to this earth, and then they will remember kindly and bless those who are living now. Oh, my dear sisters, it seems as if just a little more and we shall know why we live, why we suffer . . . If only we knew . . . If only we knew . . . " (*It is still.*) Thank you, sir. That's all I wanted. . . . You've made me very happy. . . . God bless you, sir. (*She walks off the stage. . . . The stage is empty.*)

"The Arrangement."

Narrator. ACT II. Scene iv.

This opening speech establishes the premise for a sketch about a father hiring a prostitute for his son as a means of introducing him to "manhood."

NARRATOR

. . . This one goes back a good many years ago to my youth . . . I was 19 years old to be exact . . . and in the ways of love. I was not only unschooled, I hadn't even been in the classroom. . . . I was so innocent and shy, that I actually thought that since the beginning of time, no woman had *ever* been completely unclothed. . . . As for connubial bliss, I dared not think of it. And as for impregnation, I chose to believe it was caused by the husband giving the wife a most ardent handshake before retiring . . . and let it go at that. . . . But my father was a wonderful man . . . quite liberal in his thinking and on the occasion of my 19th birthday, he decided to introduce me to the mysteries of love. He was, however, a frugal man, and decided to escort me himself, to see, in the matter of bargaining, that I would not be taken advantage of. . . . Picture me, if you will, as my own dear father . . . Antosha! . . . Antosha! Where are you? . . . Don't stand there in the dark shaking like a puppy dog. Come here. . . . We have some adolescence to get over with. . . . (*Young Anton appears,*

19 years old, as nervous as a puppy. He frets with his hat in his hand.)

"The Writer."

Narrator. ACT II. Scene v.

In this curtain speech, the Narrator (Chekhov) speaks of his love for writing and thanks the audience for sharing the products of his creative imagination.

NARRATOR

. . . I hope that portrait of my father came out with some affection. I loved him very much. . . . And yet with him, as with all the other characters I've shared with you tonight, I have a sense of betrayal. . . . When I put down my pen at the end of a day's work, I cannot help but feel that I have robbed my friends of their precious life fluid. . . . What makes my conscience torment me even more, is that I've had a wonderful time writing today . . . but before I go . . . what was it we were talking about? Early on, before the story of Cherdyakov? . . . Ahh, yes . . . I was about to say what it was, as a child, I most wanted to do with my life. Well, then—(*He thinks for a moment.*) Funny, for the life of me I can't remember . . . but somehow, as I stand here with a feeling of great peace and contentment, in some measure I suspect I must be doing it. Thank you for this visit. If ever you pass this way again, please drop in. Good night. . . . Wait! . . . There's an alternative ending. . . . If ever you pass this way again, I hope you inherit five million rubles. Good night. [Cue 12.] (*He turns and moves upstage.*)

GOD'S FAVORITE

Premièred December 11, 1974
at the Eugene O'Neill Theatre, New York City

Directed by Michael Bennett

CAST

Joe Benjamin	Vincent Gardenia
Ben Benjamin	Lawrence John Moss
Sarah Benjamin	Laura Esterman
Rose Benjamin	Maria Karnilova
David Benjamin	Terry Kiser
Mady	Rosetta LeNoire
Morris	Nick LaTour
Sidney Lipton	Charles Nelson Reilly

The action of the play takes place in the Benjamin mansion on the North Shore of Long Island.

Joe Benjamin is a fifty-six-year-old self-made man. From meager beginnings he has, with ingenuity and industry, built a dynasty from the manufacture and sales of cardboard boxes. As a result, he now lives an opulent lifestyle with his family on their Long Island Estate. Joe is a truly good man, a religious, philanthropic man who gives fifty percent of his earnings to charity. Unfortunately, he is also plagued by the profligate behavior of his eldest son, David, a boy he loves in spite of his indiscretions.

Late one evening Joe is visited by Sidney Lipton, a three-dimensional messenger of God who works for Him out of his home in Jackson Heights. He has been chosen to deliver the message that Joe is God's favorite and that God, as a test of faith, has bet the Devil that Joe is the one man in the universe who will never renounce Him.

In spite of Lipton's warnings of the pain and problems that will be visited upon him, Joe refuses to sign a renunciation. As a result, Joe's faith is sorely tested: his factory burns to the ground, his business flounders, he is beset with physical ailments that inflict excruciating pain, his mansion is razed by fire and, in a crowning blow, David goes off on a drunken binge and he is abandoned by his family. But Joe is still resolute in his refusal to renounce God.

Due to Joe's steadfastness, Joe Lipton admits defeat, the family returns, and profligate son David has an epiphany that ends his dissolute ways.

Joe. ACT I. Scene i.

Joe loves his son David in spite of his dissolute ways. When David blames his drunken, profligate behavior on wealth, Joe attempts to enlighten him. But his remarks fall on deaf ears.

JOE

This house could go up in smoke tomorrow, I wouldn't blink an eye. I'll tell you something . . . There was a time in my life when the holes in my socks were so big, you could put them on from either end . . . I grew up in a tenement in New York. My mother, my father and eleven kids in one and a half rooms. We had two beds and a cot, you had to take a number off the wall to go to sleep . . . My father was five foot three, weighed a hundred and twenty-seven pounds. He had a bad heart, bad lungs, bad liver and bad kidneys. He was a piano mover. He died at the age of thirty-two from an acute attack of everything . . . My mother had to take a job in a sweatshop working six days a week, fourteen hours a day. At night she washed floors at Madison Square Garden, and on Sundays she sold hot sweet potatoes on the corner of Fourteenth Street and Broadway. What she didn't sell was dinner for the rest of the week. Sweet potatoes every night. On Thanksgiving she'd stuff the sweet potato with a little white potato . . . The clothes we wore were made out or rags she found in the street, or a pair of curtains somebody threw away . . . You know what it is for a young boy growing up in a tough neighborhood in East New York to wear *curtains*? . . . Can you picture that? *Fairies* used to beat me up . . . And through all those freezing winters and hot, hungry summers, through all the years of scrimping and scrubbing, through sickness without doctors or medicines—one winter we all had the whooping cough at the same time, eleven kids throwing up simultaneously in one and a half rooms—my mother nursed us on roller skates . . . through all that pain and heartache and suffering, she never complained or cried out against the world, because she knew it was God's will. That was the lesson my mother taught us. "What God has given, God can take away. And for what God has given you, be thankful" . . . When I was fourteen years old I went to work for the Schreiber Corrugated Box Company. A rotten man who made a rotten box. No matter how you packed it, the minute you shipped it, it fell apart. It didn't hold up under any kind of weather—including sunshine. Because Schreiber was interested in a quick profit, not workmanship, not quality. When I bought the business from him in 1942 with six thousand dollars my mother saved, I started to make quality boxes, strong as steel. In the first three months I lost my mother's six thousand dollars. "It's God's will," she kept telling me. And then suddenly business began to pick up. From nowhere, from *everywhere*, people were buying my corrugated boxes. It was like a miracle. The money kept pouring in. I couldn't find banks fast enough to keep it . . . My mother never lived to enjoy my success . . . On the day I made my first million dollars, she died peacefully in her sleep on the BMT subway. Her last words to the conductor were, "If God wanted me to live, I would have taken the bus today." . . . All I wanted for my wife and children was not to suffer the way I did as a child, not to be deprived of life's barest necessities. But such riches, such wealth? I never asked for it, I never needed it. But when I ask myself, "Why so much, why all this?" I hear the voice of my mother say, "It's God's will" . . . I give half of what I have every year to charity, and the next year I make twice as much. Wealth is as much a responsibility as poverty is a burden. I'll accept whatever is given to me and ask for no more or no less . . . Can you understand this, David? Does anything I've said to you tonight make any sense at all? (*David snores.*) He's sleeping! Why do you torture me? Why do you twist my heart around like a pretzel? Where is your faith, David? Have I brought you up without faith, or have you just lost it?

Sidney Lipton. ACT I. Scene i.

When Joe, doubtful that Sidney Lipton is God's messenger, threatens to call the police, Lipton convinces him of his legitimacy with the following speech:

LIPTON

(*Points a long arm and finger again.*) *Stay! I stay you! I render you powerless and motionless!* (*Joe picks up the PHONE and dials.*) All right, I can't do it, but put down the phone, please. I'll tell you everything. (*Joe looks at him; puts down the receiver.*) I'll tell you what I know, take it or leave it . . . God and Satan were sitting around having one of those boring philosophical debates—this was a week ago Tuesday. And Satan was sitting there in this pink suit—gorgeous tan, little mole on his cheek . . . And Satan says there is not one man on the face of the earth, in the entire universe—regardless of race, religion, Polish, whatever—who would not renounce God once the Devil put enough heat on. Can you believe it? Two grown deities talking like this? To which *God* said—this is a quote, they got it on tape—*one* man would never renounce. And that man is . . . (*Makes a bugle sound.*) Ta tum ta tum ta tum ta tum ta taaa . . . JOE BENJAMIN! Thrills, right? . . . So they make a bet—I'm only telling you what I heard—and the bet is, the Devil will make your life so miserable, you'll renounce God! So-o-o, that's it. Hell of a story, isn't it?

CALIFORNIA SUITE

(V)

Premièred June 10, 1976
at the Eugene O'Neill Theatre, New York City

CAST
"Visitor from Philadelphia"

Marvin Michaels   Jack Weston
Bunny   Leslie Easterbrook
Millie Michaels   Barbara Barrie

CAST
"Visitors from Chicago"

Mort Hollender   Jack Weston
Beth Hollender   Barbara Barrie
Stu Franklyn   George Grizzard
Gert Franklyn   Tammy Grimes

California Suite is composed of four playlets whose action
takes place in rooms 203 and 204 in the Beverly Hills Hotel.

"Visitor from Philadelphia."

Marvin. ACT I. Scene ii.

Marvin Michaels, after a night of indiscretion, awakens to the realization that the woman is still in his bed and his wife's arrival is imminent. In a state of panic, he attempts to arouse the hooker and dispatch her before Millie Michaels makes her appearance.

MARVIN

Oh, God . . . (*He rubs his face with both hands.*) Ohhhhhhhhhhh. (*He gets up and goes into the bathroom, moving almost zombie-like as he feels the awfulness of his hangover. Marvin Michaels is about forty-two. He wears undershorts, T-shirt and* one *black sock. His hair is rumpled. We hear him gargle. He comes out of the bathroom, goes back to the bed, gets in and sits up.*) Ugh, never again . . . Never never never . . . (*He sits there trying to breathe, and suddenly, from under the sheets, a arm comes out. A female arm. He recoils, frightened to death.*) Oh, God . . . (*He lifts the hand to his face and looks at it. He lifts the cover back, and we see a woman, who, from what we can make out, seems to be attractive. She is wearing the tops of his pajamas.*) What are you doing here? I thought you left! (*There is no response from her: she is out like a light.*) Hey! (*He nudges her.*) Hey, come on, you can't stay here! Hey, wake up! (*He turns, gropes for his watch on the night table, and looks at it.*) Eleven o'clock! Jesus Christ, it's eleven o'clock! (*He jumps out of bed.*) Wake up! Come on, get up, it's eleven o'clock, don't you understand? (*He turns back and reaches for the PHONE.*) Crazy! I must be crazy! (*Into the PHONE.*) Operator? . . . What time is it? . . . (*Screams.*) Eleven o'clock? . . . Why didn't you call me? . . . I left a wake-up call for eight o'clock . . . I *did!* . . . Mr. Michaels, Room 203, an eight o'clock wake-up call . . . *I didn't!* . . . I can't understand that . . .

Never mind, did I get any calls? . . . Well, take the hold signal off, I'm taking calls. (*He hangs up.*) How could I forget to leave a wake-up call? (*He nudges the girl, then starts getting dressed.*) Hey, come on. Get up, will ya? You have to get dressed. My wife could walk in any minute. Eleven o'clock—her plane probably got in already. (*He gets his pants and other sock on.*) *Will you get up? We got an emergency here!* (*He puts his shirt on. The girl hasn't moved.*) What's wrong with you? You deaf or something? (*He crosses to the bed. She is breathing but not moving.*) Are you all right? (*He nudges her again. She moans but doesn't move. He turns and looks at the floor next to the bed, and picks up a quart-size empty bottle of vodka.*) Oh, God, what did you do? An entire bottle of vodka? You drank a whole bottle of vodka with my wife coming in? Are you crazy? (*He nudges her.*) Are you all right? Can you hear me? (*She moans.*) What? What did you say? . . . I couldn't hear that. (*She moans again. He puts his ear to her mouth.*) Sick . . . You feel sick? . . . Six margaritas and a bottle of vodka, I wonder why . . . Listen, you can get dressed and take a cab home and be nice and sick in your own bed all day . . . Doesn't that sound nice? Heh? (*There is no response.*) Oh, God, what am I going to do? . . . Water. You want a little water? (*He rushes to the table, pour a glass of ice water and rushes back to her.*) Here, lady. Sip a little cold water. (*He picks her head up and tries to pour some water into her mouth, but her lips won't open and it dribbles down her face.*) Drink, sweetheart . . . for my sake . . . Open your lips, you crazy broad! (*To himself.*) Don't panic . . . Panic is the quickest way to divorce . . . mustn't panic! (*He sticks his fingers in the glass and flicks water at her face.*) Up, up, up! Here we go! Rise and shine, everybody up! (*He throws more water. She doesn't budge. He shakes her shoulders—she flops about like a ragdoll.*) Move! Please, God, make her move. I'll never be a bad person again as long as I live. (*She doesn't move; she lies there.*) All right, we're gonna get you dressed and down into a cab. Once you're on your feet, you'll be fine . . . I'm really sorry this happened. I don't remember much, but it must have been a wonderful evening, whatever your name is . . . Could you help me a little, honey? Please? . . . You're not gonna help me. All right, Marvin, think. Think, Marvin. (*He slaps his own face to help him think.*) I gotta get outta here. (*He picks up the PHONE.*) Operator, get me the front desk. (*He looks at the girl, Bunny.*) I have two wonderful children who need a father— don't do this to me. (*Into the PHONE.*) Hello? . . . This is an *angry* Mr. Michaels in Suite 203 and 4 . . . Listen, I am very uncomfortable in my room . . . The toilet kept dripping all night. No, I don't want it fixed. I want another room. I could move out immediately . . . I'm expecting my wife in from Philadelphia any minute, and I *know* she's not going to be happy once she sees this room . . . *Who's* here? . . . MY WIFE? MY-WIFE-IS-HERE? . . . You sent my wife up without calling me? . . . How could you do such a thing? What the hell kind of a cheap hotel are you running here? . . . Can't you send someone to stop her? She's not going to like this room! (*There is a knock on the living room door. He slams the PHONE down and dashes around the room in a frenzy.*) Oh, God! (*Whispers to the inert form.*) Oh, God! Oh, God! OH, GOD! OH, GOD! OH, GOD! Listen to me . . . I have to go into the other room. When I'm inside, lock the door from in here. Don't open it for anyone, do you understand? . . . For anyone! (*Another knock on the door. He goes into living room, closing bedroom door. Then asks softly and innocently.*) Who is it?

"Visitors from Chicago."

Stu. ACT II. Scene iii.

After traveling together for three weeks, the Hollenders' and Franklyns' tolerance for each other has grown precariously thin. And when Beth Hollender injures her ankle during a overly-competi-

tive tennis match with the Franklyns that Mort Hollender describes as a "war," buried hostility erupts in a paroxysm of verbal and physical abuse. Here Stu Franklyn vents his frustrations:

STU

You call this a vacation? I had a better vacation when I had my hernia operation . . . I'm sick of your face. I'm sick of your twelve-cent cigars. After three weeks, my clothes smell like they've been in a humidor. I'm sick of your breakfasts. I'm sick of you lightly buttered rye toast and eggs over lightly every goddamned morning. Would it kill you to have a waffle once in a while? One stinkin' little waffle for my sake?

Intervening speech. Mort: What are you, crazy? We got two invalids in bed and you're talking about waffles?

STU (*cont'd.*)

We did everything *you* wanted. *You* made all the decisions. You took *all* the pictures. I didn't get to take *one* picture with my own camera. You picked all the restaurants—nine Japanese restaurants in three weeks. I am nauseated at the sight of watching you eat tempura with your shoes off. I am bored following your wife into every chatska store on the West Coast looking for Mexican bracelets—

Intervening speech. Mort: Hey, hey, wait a minute. Your wife bought too. What about a pair of African earrings that hang down to her navel?

STU (*cont'd.*)

A year I planned for this vacation. You know what I got to show for it? Two purple Hawaiian shirts for *my* kids that *you* picked out. Even *Hawaiians* wouldn't wear them. One entire morning wasted in Honolulu while five Chinese tailors measured you for a thirty-nine-dollar Hong Kong suit that fell apart in the box. I spent half an after-noon on Fisherman's Wharf watching a near-sighted eighty-four-year-old artist sketching a charcoal portrait of you that looks like Charles Laughton. I've had enough! I want to go home! I'm a nervous wreck . . . I need a vacation.

CHAPTER TWO

Premièred on December 4, 1977
at the Imperial Theatre, New York City

Directed by Herbert Ross

CAST

George Schneider	Judd Hirsch
Leo Schneider	Cliff Gorman
Jennie Malone	Anita Gillette
Faye Medwick	Ann Wedgeworth

The action of the play takes place in Jennifer Malone's upper East Side apartment and George Schneider's lower Central Park West apartment.

George Schneider is a forty-two-year-old writer living a dour, monastic existence since losing Barbara, his wife of twelve years. His concerned older brother, Leo, an unhappily married womanizer, is determined to find George companionship and arranges a series of ridiculous liaisons before recommending that he meet Jennie Malone, a divorced actress he has met through their mutual friend Faye Medwick. George resists the meeting as does Jennie, who is still suffering the aftershocks of a very bad former marriage. But an accidental phone call from George results in them getting together for a quick, noncommittal "look." The "look," however, proves to be to their mutual satisfaction, and after a whirlwind romance of two weeks, and over Leo's objections, they decide to marry.

Leo's unheeded warnings that George was not ready for marriage seems prophetic when George and Jennie return from their honeymoon in a state of acrimony. George cannot overcome the deep-seated psychological impediment of accepting happiness because doing so would mean that he would have to let go of Barbara. Rather than facing the problem, George accepts a writing assignment on The Coast as a means of running. But Jennie is committed. She loves George and won't give him up without a fight. Her strength and solidarity make George realize how much he loves and needs her, and gives him the courage to put Barbara behind him and face happiness without fear.

The subplot, which greatly strengthens the message of the main story, involves an affair between the womanizing Leo and married Faye. Here, in diametric contrast to George and Jennie, is a portrait of people floundering, attempting to find happiness without real love and commitment.

Leo. ACT I. Scene ix.

George is ecstatic after finally making an emotional connection with another woman after his wife's untimely death, but his brother, Leo, is in a deep funk because his marriage is on the verge of collapse. Here, Leo relates his feelings about the suffocating and mundane state of his connubial situation.

Preceding speech. George: Come on, Leo. You've got a good marriage—*I know.*

LEO

Really? I'll invite you to sleep in our bedroom one night, you can listen. I'll tell you, George. The trouble with marriage is that it's relentless. Every morning when you wake up, it's still there. If I could just get a leave of absence every once in a while. A two-week leave of absence. I used to get them all the time in the Army, and I always came back . . . I don't know. I think it was different for you and Barbara. I'll tell you the truth, I always thought the two of you were a little crazy. But that's what made it work for you. You had a real bond of lunacy between you . . . Marilyn has no craziness. No fantasies. No uncharted territories to explore. I'm sitting there with maps for places in my mind I've never been, and she won't even pack an overnight bag. In eleven years she never once let me make love to her with the lights on. I said to her, "Marilyn, come on, trust me, I won't tell anybody." So we stop growing, stop changing. And we stagnate . . . in our comfortable little house in the country . . . Oh, well, another thirty, thirty-five years and it'll be over, right? (*He sits back.*) All right, I've told someone. I feel better . . . Now, what the hell is it you feel so wonderful about?

Leo. ACT II. Scene ii.

After knowing each other for just two weeks, George and Jennie have decided to marry. Leo, as a protective older brother, feels that the decision is impulsive, fraught with disastrous potentials, and begs George to put some time in the relationship. When he asks George's permission to speak with Jennie, George grants it because he is confident that Jennie will allay his trepidation, which she does after this graphic speech regarding George's fragile state following his wife's death.

LEO

(*Thinks, takes his time.*) All right . . . They were very close. I mean, as close as any couple I've ever seen. After ten years, they still held hands in a restaurant. I'm married eleven years and I don't pass the salt to my wife . . . When George first found out how ill Barbara was, he just refused to accept it. He knew it was serious, but there was no way she was not going to beat it. He just couldn't conceive of it. And Barbara never let on to a soul that anything was ever wrong. Her best friend, at the funeral, said to George, "I just didn't know" . . . She was beautiful, Jennie, in every way. And then in the last few months you could see she was beginning to slip. George would go out to dinner or a party and leave early, trying not to let on that anything was wrong—and especially not letting on to themselves . . . And then one morning George called me from the hospital, and he said very quietly and simply, "She's gone, Leo." And it surprised me because I thought when it was finally over, George would go to pieces. I mean, I expected a full crackup, and it worried me that he was so held together . . . I saw him as often as I could, called him all the time, and then suddenly I didn't hear from him for about five days. He didn't answer the phone. I called the building. They said they didn't see him go in or out, and I got plenty scared. I went up there—they let me in with the passkey—and I found him in the bedroom sitting in front of the television set, with the picture on and no sound. He was in filthy pajamas, drenched in perspiration. There was a container of milk on the floor next to him that had gone sour. He must have dropped eight or nine pounds. And I said to him, "Hey, George, why don't you answer your phone? Are you okay." And he said, "Fine, I'm fine, Leo." Then he reached over and touched my hand, and for the first time in a year and a half, the real tears started to flow. He cried for hours—through that whole night. I still couldn't get him to eat, so the next morning I got our doctor to come over, and he checked him into Mount Sinai. He was there for ten days. And he was in terrible shape. His greatest fear was that I was going to commit him someplace. When he came out, he stayed with me about a week. I couldn't even get him to take a walk. He had this panic, this fear he'd never make it back into the house. I finally got him to walk down to the corner, and he never let go of my arm for a second. We started across the street and he stopped and said, "No, it's too far. Take me back, Leo." A few weeks later he went into therapy. A really good doctor. He was there about a month, then suddenly decided he wasn't going back. He wouldn't explain why. I called the doctor and he explained to me that George was making a very determined effort not to get better. Because getting better meant he was ready to let go of Barbara, and there was no way he was going to let that happen. And then one day, bang, he took off for Europe. But not new places. Only the ones he'd visited with Barbara before. When he came back, he looked better, seemed more cheerful. So in my usual dumb, impulsive way, I figured he would want what I would want if I were in his place—companionship. Well, companionship to him and me, I found out, were two different things. But he has good instincts. He knows what's right for him. And God knows what I offered wasn't right . . . until the night I saw you sitting there with Faye and I said, "Oh yeah, that's for George." I swear to you, Jennie, you are the best thing that could happen to that man. I was just hoping it would happen a little later . . . I'm sorry. No matter how I say all this, it doesn't seem to come out right. But you wanted to hear it. I just felt I had an obligation to say it. I hope you understand that, Jennie.

Jennie. ACT II. Scene vii.

Jennie and George have recently returned from their honeymoon, and already their marriage is in serious trouble because George, still bound to the past, will not accept happiness because accepting happiness would mean having to let go of Barbara. Psychologically unwilling to break free, George has taken an assignment in Los Angeles as a means of running from the problem. Although Jennie is threatened by George's leaving, she has found her center, feels good about herself, and is committed to fighting for their marriage.

JENNIE

You know what you want better than me, George . . . I don't know what you expect to find out there, except a larger audience for your two shows a day of suffering . . . I know I'm not as smart as you. Maybe I can't analyze and theorize and speculate on why we behave as we do and react as we do and suffer guilt and love and hate. You read all those books, not me . . . But there's one thing I *do* know. I know how I *feel.* I know I can stand here watching you try to destroy everything I've ever wanted in my life, wanting to smash your face with my fists because you won't even make the slightest effort to opt for happiness—and still know that I love you. That's always so clear to me. It's the one place I get all my strength from . . . You mean so much to me that I am willing to take all your abuse and insults and insensitivity—because that's what you need to do to prove I'm not going to leave you. I can't promise I'm not going to die, George, that's asking too much. But if you want to test me, go ahead and test me. You want to leave, leave! But *I'm* not the one who's going to walk away. I don't know if I can take it forever, but I can take if for tonight and I can take it next week. Next month I may be a little shaky . . . But I'll tell you something, George. No matter what you say about me, I feel so good about myself—better than I felt when I ran from Cleveland and was frightened to death of New York. Better than I felt when Gus was coming home at two o'clock in the morning just to change his clothes. Better than I felt when I thought there was no one in the world out there for me, and better than I felt the night before we got married and I thought that I wasn't good enough for you . . . Well, I am! I'm wonderful! I'm nuts about me! And if you're stupid enough to throw someone sensational like me aside, then you don't deserve as good as you've got! I am sick and tired of running from places and people and relationships . . . And don't tell me what I want because *I'll* tell you what I want. I want a home and I want a family—and I want a career, too. And I want a dog and I want a cat and I want three goldfish. I want *everything*! There's no harm in wanting it, George, because there's not a chance in hell we're going to get it all, anyway. But if you don't *want* it, you've got even less chance than that . . . Everyone's out there looking for easy answers. And if you don't find it at home, hop into another bed and maybe you'll come up lucky. *Maybe*! You'd be just as surprised as me at some of the "maybe's" I've seen out there lately. Well, none of that for me, George . . . You want me, than fight for me, because I'm fighting like hell for you. I think we're both worth it. I will admit, however, that I *do* have one fault. One glaring, major, monumental fault . . . Sometimes I don't know when to stop talking. For that I'm sorry, George, and I apologize. I am now through! (*She sits back on the sofa, exhausted.*)

I OUGHT to BE in PICTURES

Premièred April 3, 1980
at the Eugene O'Neill Theatre, New York City

Directed by Herbert Ross

CAST

Libby	Dinah Manoff
Steffy	Joyce Van Patten
Herb	Ron Liebman

The action of the play takes place in a small bungalow in West Hollywood, California.

Herb Tucker is a down-on-his-luck scriptwriter living in a run-down rental in West Hollywood. He hasn't been productive for some time and rationalizes that the state of the industry is the reason he isn't connecting. In truth, he has become an unmotivated procrastinator with a defeatist attitude. Herb's longtime, sleep-over girlfriend is Steffy Blondell, an attractive forty-year-old who is a make-up artist at Columbia Pictures. She is Herb's anchor and friend and attempts, to no avail, to motivate him and boost his confidence.

When Herb's nineteen-year-old daughter, Libby, arrives unexpectedly from New York, they are unable to relate; he hasn't seen her for sixteen years since he walked out on his wife, Libby, and his son, Robby. Libby tells Herb that she has come to the Coast to get into pictures, but in truth she is there because she is bereft of love and desperately needs to make a familial connection. But it is difficult for Herb to give of himself and make commitments, an aspect of his personality that has also become a problem for Steffy, who wants more than the occasional night in his bed.

Libby, a self-sufficient girl, moves into the bungalow and transforms it from a depressing environment to one that is bright and cheerful. She can apparently do anything. She even tunes up Herb's old Mustang. Then she wrangles a job as a valet, parking cars for Hollywood's rich and famous. When Herb takes her to task for her pipe dream of being a movie star, she retaliates, rightfully accusing him of being a negative procrastinator. The ensuing conflict climaxes with Libby spilling her real feelings—she wants to be unconditionally loved. This results in a touching scene during which father and daughter open the floodgates of true emotion.

Libby, haven gotten the emotional support she came for, announces that she is returning to New York. Then in a crowning maneuver, during a phone call home, she prods Herb into speaking with her mother and his son, Robby. Then she departs as she came—unceremoniously, leaving in her wake an enlightened Herb.

Libby. ACT I. Scene i.

Herb Tucker has not seen his daughter Libby since he walked out on his wife and family sixteen years ago. Now Libby unexpectedly shows up on his doorstep. After an initial period of small talk, their conversation turns rancorous when Herb is not supportive of Libby's request that he help launch her career in show business.

LIBBY

(*To her father.*) Well, let me tell you something, Mr. Herbert Tucker. The one who hasn't made it in show business is you, not me. I'm on the way up on the local and you're on the way-down express. It's possible, just possible, that one day I may be standing up there getting my Emmy Award or my Grammy or my Oscar or whatever the hell they get out here. And I'm going to smile and say to the entire world, "I want to thank everyone who helped me win this award. My grandmother, my mother, my brother Robby, my friends, my fans and everyone else except my shitheel father. I think that about covers it!" . . . I apologize for my language, Steffy. It was very nice meeting you. I'm sorry I can't say that for everyone else in this house. (*She starts for the door. Herb catches her.*)

Herb. ACT I. Scene i.

This is Herb's response to Libby's speech above.

HERB

(*Angrily.*) Wait a minute, you! You just listen to me a minute. I never figured I had anything coming to me. I gave you up, that was *my* loss. I left that house because if I had stayed it would have turned into a war zone and there would have been *no* survivors. You want to talk about guilts, regrets—I got enough to fill up my garage. But that's my business and I'll handle it my own way. I never expected anything from you *or* your brother. Outside this house, you can call me any goddamn thing you want to call me. But under this roof is my domain, and if you talk to me, you show me some respect.

Herb. ACT I. Scene ii.

Driven by a mix of contrition and caring, Herb has retrieved Libby after she ran from the house during a bitter exchange between them. He offers her lodging and understanding and does his best to explain his reasons for leaving home in the following speech

HERB

The truth is, I didn't like her very much . . . Oh, she was a good woman. Worked hard, never complained when we didn't have enough money . . . The trouble was, she wasn't any fun. She had no humor at all. I could never make her laugh. That's what hurt me more than anything. We'd go to a party, I'd have a couple of drinks, in an hour, I swear, I'd have them all rolling on the floor. And I'd look over at her and she's just be staring at me. A blank look on her face. Not angry, not upset, just not understanding. As if she walked into a foreign movie that didn't have any subtitles. She just didn't know how to enjoy herself. Oh, I know where it all came from. You're poor, you grow up in the Depression, life means struggle, hard work, responsibilities. I came from the same background, but we always laughed in my house. Didn't have meat too often, but we had fun. Her father never went to a movie, never went to a play. He only danced *once* in his entire life, at his wedding—and he did *that* because it was custom, tradition, not joy, not happiness. I give him a book to read and if he found in the middle he was enjoying it, he would put it down. Education, yes. Entertainment, no . . . Anyway, we were married about four years, and one day I was just sitting there eating her mushroom and barley soup, which happened to be delicious, and I decided I didn't want any more. Not the soup—my life. So I went inside, packed my bags and said, "Blanche, I think I got to get out of here. And I don't think I'm ever coming back" . . . And I swear to you, Libby, if she had laughed I would have stayed. If she saw the craziness of what I was doing, the absurdity of it, I would have unpacked my bags and finished my soup. But she looked at me, cold as ice, and said, "If that's how you feel, who wants you?" So I put on my hat, left her whatever cash I had in my pocket, walked down the stairs and I never came back . . . And that's it. As simple as that.

Herb. ACT II. Scene iii.

Libby has moved in with Herb and has done wonders for the household. She has cleaned, painted, and spruced up the place in general. She is a whiz. She is also upbeat and positive—not a defeatist like Herb.

During the past few evenings, Libby has been returning home at all hours. Herb, displaying the tendencies of a normal father, is deeply concerned for her well-being. Upon questioning, he learns that she has taken a job as a parking attendant, and that she is using the position as a means of advertising her acting talent to influential people on the Hollywood scene—she writes her message on the back of their parking tickets. Unable to see that she is showing the tenacity and grit that he lacks, Herb derides her enterprising idea as a foolish waste of time.

HERB

YOU HAVE *NO* CHANCE! NONE! There are five thousand qualified agents in this town who can't get their clients a meeting with these people, but *you* think they're going to call *you* because *you* left *your* name on the back of a stub they're going to throw out the window the minute they pull out of the driveway?

Intervening speech. Libby: That's a very pessimistic attitude to take.

HERB (*cont'd.*)

(*Trying to control himself.*) Okay! For the sake of argument, let us say someone looks at the card. Someone is looking for a valet service for his son's bar mitzvah. Someone just met a girl at the party and wants to write down her number. Someone has a piece of spare rib in his teeth and is trying to pick it out with the card. Only a small percentage of *that* group will look at the back of the card. But let's say one does. He sees, "Libby Tucker, New York trained actress—No Part Is Too Big or Too Small." Do you imagine he's going to slam his foot on the brake, pull off the road and, say to his wife, "That's exactly what I'm looking for. An actress trained in New York who doesn't care if her part is too big or too small. Right under my nose in my very own car. What a break for me. I'll contact her first thing in the morning and hope and pray that someone else with spare ribs in their teeth didn't get to her before me!"

Libby. ACT II. Scene iii.

In this speech immediately following Herb's above, Libby offers a cogent response to his negativity.

LIBBY

If I stayed in Brooklyn, I never would have come out here. If I never came out here, I never would have met Steffy. If I didn't meet Steffy, she never would have told me about the Los Angeles Academy of Dramatic Arts. If I didn't go over to the Los Angeles Academy of Dramatic Arts, I never would have met Gordon Zaharias of Peoria,

Illinois. If I didn't meet Gordon Zaharias, I never would have gotten a job driving George Segal's car. If I didn't drive all those big shots' cars, the name and number of Libby Tucker would never be stuck in their windshields. Where is *your* number stuck? If you don't pick yourself up and do something in this world, they bury you in Mount Hebron Cemetery and on you tombstone it says, "Born 1906—Died 1973 . . . and in between HE DIDN'T DO NOTHIN'"!

Libby. ACT II. Scene iii.

Libby reveals her innermost feelings. Although outwardly composed and confident, she is riddled with insecurities due to feelings of abandonment and not being loved. She feels that she has always been used as a surrogate through which people could express their love for others.

LIBBY

Confidence? . . . I'm scared from the minute I wake up every morning.

Intervening speech. Herb: Of what?

LIBBY (*cont'd.*)

Of everything. I get up an hour before you just to check if you're still there . . . I know Grandma's dead. I know she probably can't hear me. But I speak to her every day anyway because I'm not so sure anyone else is listening. If I have to go for an interview, my heart pounds so much you can see it coming through my blouse. That thing about writing my name on the valet stubs? It wasn't my idea. It was Gordon's. He did it first, so I just copied him . . . If you want the God's honest truth, I don't even want to be an actress. I don't know the first thing about acting. I don't know *what* I want to be . . .

(*Beginning to break down.*) I just wanted to come out here and see you. I just wanted to know what you were like. I wanted to know why I was so frightened every time a boy wanted to reach out and touch me . . . I just wanted somebody in the family to hold me because it was *me*, Libby, and not somebody who wasn't there. . .

FOOLS

Premièred on April 6, 1981
at the Eugene O'Neill Theatre, New York City

Directed by Mike Nichols

CAST

Leon Tolchinsky	John Rubinstein
Snetsky	Gerald Hiken
Magistrate	Fred Stuthman
Slovitch	David Lipman
Mishkin	Joseph Leon
Yenchna	Florence Stanley
Dr. Zubritsky	Harold Gould
Lenya Zubritsky	Mary Louise Wilson
Sophia Zubritsky	Pamela Reed
Gregor Yousekevitch	Richard B. Shull

The action of the play takes place in the town of Kulyenchikov in the year 1890.

Leon Tolchinsky is ecstatic. He has landed a terrific job as a schoolteacher in the idyllic Russian hamlet of Kulyenchikov. But when he arrives, he finds people sweeping dust from the stoops *back into* their homes, and people who think that if you milk a cow upside down, you get more cream. Kulyenchikov, it seems, has been cursed with chronic stupidity for two hundred years, and the desperate townspeople have hired Leon, hoping he can break the curse. But they don't tell him that if he stays more than twenty-four hours—and fails to break the curse—he also becomes stupid. Why doesn't Leon leave, you say? Because he has fallen in love with the beautiful daughter of the town doctor. She is so stupid she that has only recently learned how to sit down. Of course, Leon breaks the curse and gets the girl.

Leon. ACT I. Scene i.

This speech opens the play and is directed to the audience. Leon Tolchinsky arrives in Kulyenchikov carrying a battered old suitcase and some books tied together. He looks around, seemingly pleased with what he sees. The speech is interrupted by arrival of Snetsky the shepherd.

LEON

(*Smiles.*) Kulyenchikov, I like it! It's exactly as I pictured: a quiet, pleasant village, not too large . . . the perfect place for a new schoolteacher to begin his career . . . Well, to be honest, I did spend mornings for two years in a small children's school in Moscow teaching tiny tots rudimentary spelling and numbers, but this, *this* is my first bona-fide, professional appointment as a full-time school-master. Actually, I never heard of Kulyenchikov until I saw the advertisement that a Dr. Zubritsky placed in the college journal. Although the position was in a remote village in the Ukraine, I jumped at the chance, but I don't mind telling you that my heart is pounding with excitement. I have this passion for teaching . . . Greek, Latin, astronomy, classic literature. I get goose bumps just thinking about it . . . (*He looks around.*) I don't see anyone around . . . Maybe I arrived a little early—I'm one of those extremely eager and enthusiastic people who's up at the crack of dawn, ready to begin his work. This is a very, very auspicious day in my life. (*We hear a ram's horn off-stage.*) Oh! Excuse me.

Leon. ACT II. Scene ii.

The marriage of Leon and Sophia breaks the curse of stupidity and the citizenry of Kulyenchikov are now enlightened and intelligent. In this curtain speech, Leon introduces the cast of characters, explaining how each has been transformed.

LEON

(*To the audience. During his speech, the cast members appear as he mentions them.*) When you think of it, it's not such a bizarre story, after all. Be honest. Haven't you all met someone in your life who came from a place like Kulyenchikov? An aunt, an uncle, a neighbor . . . your boss! Of course, once the curse was lifted, we became like any other small town or village in any other part of the world, susceptible to all the "ups and down" of normal life—well, the magistrate, for example. (*The Magistrate appears.*) After two more years in office, greed got the better part of him and he was convicted for taking bribes for political favors. He served two years in jail and eventually sold his memoirs for a fortune. (*Mishkin appears.*) Mishkin gave up the postal service and became a writer. He wrote a six-hundred-page story about the Curse of Kulyenchikov and sent it off to a publisher. Unfortunately, it got lost in the mail. (*Yenchna appears.*) Yenchna, a shrewd business woman, put all her money in real estate and now owns seventeen houses in Kulyenchikov, including Count Gregor's. And as an investment for the future, she bought land in six other towns that had curses on them. (*Slovitch appears.*) Slovitch, with all his life savings, bought four more butcher shops in a village that really needed only one and went bankrupt in a month, confirming his greatest fears that with or without a curse, he didn't have much brains. (*Snetsky appears, walks like a dandy.*) Snetsky, with his newly acquired intelligence, found his sheep, gathered his wool, and became a wealthy philanthropist. (*Gregor appears in a Monk's robe.*) Count Yousekevitch became more and more lovable, studied theology, and is now the local monk. During the drought season he goes up on the hill and prays to God to throw water down on us. (*Leyna appears, looking officious.*) My dear mother-in-law, Mrs.

Zubritsky, suddenly found a voice of her own. She became the first woman mayor of Kulyenchikov and eventually consul governor of the Northern Ukraine Sector. Her husband sees her by appointment only. (*The Doctor appears.*) Dr. Zubritsky became one of the finest doctors in all of Russia. He became the personal physician to the royal family and was recently elected to the Academy of Sciences. However, he still has trouble opening jars. (*Sophia appears, carrying a baby.*) As for Sophia, she was—and still is—a miracle. Not that we don't have our differences, not that all our days are blissfully happy, but she has a wisdom that can never be found in books. She has, in turn, become my teacher, and I have learned there is no spirit on earth, evil or otherwise, that can destroy a pure heart of devoted love. As for myself, I remained a schoolmaster and dedicated my life to the education of the unenlightened . . . After all, there are so many Kulyenchikovs in this world.

BRIGHTON BEACH MEMOIRS
(V L)

Premièred December 2, 1982
at the Alvin Theatre, New York City

Directed by Gene Saks

CAST

Eugene	Matthew Broderick
Blanche	Joyce Van Patten
Kate	Elizabeth Franz
Laurie	Mandy Ingber
Nora	Jodi Thelen
Stanley	Zeljko Ivanek
Jack	Peter Michael Goetz

The action of the play takes place in a home in Brighton Beach, Brooklyn, New York.

Through the narrative of Eugene Jerome, a fifteen-year-old aspiring writer, we learn of family events taking place in his Brighton Beach home in September 1937. Other than Eugene, the household is inhabited by his mother and father, Kate and Jack Jerome, his older brother, Stan, and his aunt, Blanche, and her two daughters, Kate and Nora, who have been living with the Jeromes since the untimely death of Blanche's husband. Kate Jerome is a no-nonsense workhorse who runs the household with business-like efficiently. Husband Jack is a beleaguered but benevolent provider who works two jobs in order to eke out enough money to support the brood. Stan is a good son with a strong sense of independence and who is worshipped by Eugene, who views him as worldly-wise. Blanche, Kate's younger sister, is a pretty but frail asthmatic who lives in a state of suspended self-pity and is catered to by ever-resilient Kate. Blanche's older daughter, Nora, is an attractive, stage-struck sixteen-year-old who feels constricted and unloved. And her younger daughter, Laurie, is a pampered, sickly child whose major illness is probably hypochondria.

Conflicts ignite this volatile mix when Blanche refuses to allow Nora to appear in a Broadway musical, Stanley is threatened with losing his much-needed job, and Blanche agrees to have dinner with a neighborhood alcoholic. Then, further exacerbating matters, Jack loses his part-time job and suffers a mild heart attack.

Eugene humorously chronicles and comments upon the events that are afflicting his Brighton Beach boyhood: Nora is not speaking to Blanche for refusing to allow her to participate in show business. She also misses her father, and she resents Blanche for her preferential treatment of the "sickly" Laurie. Jack is recuperating from his heart problem and needs rest and attention at a time when finances are desperately low. Kate is disturbed that, over her objections, Blanche is planning to date a man of dubious character, and when Stan loses his critical paycheck in a poker game and leaves home as a result, she emotionally unravels in an outburst, during which she accuses Blanche of being an ungrateful malingerer.

Even though the argument between Blanche and Kate is a bitter one, it ultimately has positive, cathartic effects. Blanche is awakened, and in a confrontation with Nora she exhibits new-found insight and strength. With the air now cleared, Blanche and Kate reconcile on a level of mutual understanding. And Stanley returns, unable to walk out on his family during time of crisis.

The end of the play finds the family preparing to accept Jack's cousin and his family, refugees from war-torn Poland, into their crowded quarters. Humanity abounds in Eugene's humble Brighton Beach home.

Eugene. ACT I.

Eugene, an aspiring young writer, is chronicling the events of family life in Brighton Beach. He has just overheard a conversation between his mother and Aunt Blanche, during which his mother alluded to Blanche's "situation." As a means of clarifying this, Eugene, as he does frequently throughout the play, speaks directly to the audience.

EUGENE

(*Writing, says aloud.*) "That's-what-they-have-gutters-for" . . . (*To audience.*) If my mother knew I was writing all this down, she would stuff me like one of her chickens . . . I'd better explain what she meant by Aunt Blanche's "situation" . . . You see, her husband, Uncle Dave, died six years ago from . . . (*He looks around.*) . . . this thing . . . They never say the word. They always whisper it. It was— (*He whispers.*)—Cancer! . . . I think they're afraid if they said it out loud, God would say, "I HEARD THAT! YOU SAID THE DREAD DISEASE! (*He points finger down.*) JUST FOR THAT, I SMITE YOU DOWN WITH IT!" . . . There are some things that grownups just won't discuss . . . For example, my grandfather. He died from— (*He whispers.*)—Diphtheria! . . . Anyway, after Uncle Dave died, he left Aunt Blanche with no money. Not even insurance . . . And she couldn't support herself because she has—(*He whispers.*)—Asthma . . . So my big-hearted mother insisted we take her and her kids in to live with us. So they broke up our room into two small rooms and me and my brother Stan live on this side, and Laurie and her Sister Nora live on the other side. My father thought it would just be temporary but it's been three and a half years so far and I think because of Aunt Blanche's situation, my father is developing—(*He whispers.*)—High blood pressure!

Nora. ACT I.

Nora, Blanche's pretty sixteen-year-old daughter, has just been chosen to appear in a musical that will ultimately be produced on Broadway. She is ecstatic and has returned home in a much elevated state to impart the good news to the family.

NORA

(*A little breathless.*) Okay! Here goes! . . . I'm going to be in a Broadway show! (*They look at her in stunned silence.*) It's a musical called *Abracadabra* . . . This man, Mr. Beckman, he's a producer, came to our dancing class this afternoon and he picked out three girls. We have to be at the Hudson Theater on Monday morning at ten o'clock to audition for the dance director. But on the way out he took me aside and said the job was good as mine. I have to call him tomorrow. I may have to go into town to talk to him about it. They start rehearsing a week from Monday and then it goes to Philadelphia, Wilmington and Washington . . . and then it comes to New York the second week in December. There are nine big musical numbers and there's going to be a big tank on the stage that you can see through and the big finale all takes place with the entire cast all under water . . . I mean, can you believe it? I'm going to be in a Broadway show, Momma! (*They are all still stunned.*)

Nora. ACT I.

Nora's enthusiasm for appearing in a Broadway musical is not shared by her mother, Blanche. She rightly feels that Nora is too young and naive and that getting a proper education is paramount. But she has not given her decision. Rather, due to the fact that her brother-in-law Jack is the head of the household, she has relinquished her authority to him. Nora's fate rests in Jack's hands.

Nora, beside herself with frustration, resents having her destiny in the hands of her uncle. Here, in a scene with her younger sister, Laurie, she expresses her lingering sense of loss for her father and her commitment to the realization of a better life.

NORA

Oh, God, he was so handsome. Always dressed so dapper, his shoes always shined. I always thought he should have been a movie star . . . like Gary Cooper . . . only very short. Mostly I remember his pockets.

Intervening speech. Laurie: His pockets?

NORA (*cont'd.*)

When I was six or seven he always brought me home a little surprise. Like a Hershey or a top. He'd tell me to go get it in his coat pocket. So I'd run to the closet and put my hand in and it felt as big as a tent. I wanted to crawl in there and go to sleep. And there were all these terrific things in there, like Juicy Fruit gum or Spearmint Life Savers and bits of cellophane and crumbled pieces of tobacco and movie stubs and nickels and pennies and rubber bands and paper clips and his grey suede gloves that he wore in the wintertime.

Intervening speech. Laurie: With the stitched lines down the fingers. I remember.

NORA (*cont'd.*)

Then I found his coat in Mom's closet and I put my hand in the pocket. And everything was gone. It was emptied and dry cleaned and it felt cold . . . And that's when I knew he was really dead. (*Thinks a moment.*) Oh God, I wish we had our own place to live. I hate being a boarder. Listen, let's make a pact . . . The first one who makes enough money promises not to spend any on herself, but saves it all to get a house for you and me and Mom. That means every penny we get from now on, we save for the house . . . We can't buy *anything*. No lipstick or magazines or nail polish or bubble bum. *Nothing* . . . Is it a pact?

Kate. ACT II.

Plus the usual household burden, Kate has been undergoing added stress due to Jack's recent heart attack. Then she learns that eldest son Stan has lost his much-needed wages in a poker game. She is at the breaking point, and when Blanche accuses her of not being sympathetic to others in trouble, her pent-up feelings burst in the following verbal torrent:

KATE

You! Celia! Poppa, when he was sick. Everybody! . . . Don't you ask *me* what people! How many beatings from Momma did I get for things that you did? How many dresses did I go without so you could look like someone when you went out? I was the workhorse and you were the pretty one. You have no right to talk to me like that. No right.

Intervening speech: Blanche: This is all about Jack, isn't it? You're blaming me for what happened?

KATE (*cont'd.*)

Why do you think that man is sick today? Why did a policeman have to carry him home at two o'clock in the morning? So your Nora could have dancing lessons? So that Laurie could see a doctor every three weeks? Go on! Worry about your friend across the street, not

the ones who have to be dragged home to keep a roof over your head.
(*She turns away. Jack walks in from the kitchen.*)

JACK. ACT II.

*Jack has walked in on the confrontation between the sisters. When
Blanche, hurt by Kate's attack, announces that she can no longer
comfortably live under their roof, Jack attempts to calm emotions
and prevent a schism.*

JACK

Blanche, stop this! Stop it right now. What the hell is going on here,
for God's sake. Two sisters having a fight they should have had
twenty-five years ago. You want to get it out, Blanche, get it out!
Tell her what it's like to live in a house that isn't yours. To have to
depend on somebody else to put the food on your plate every night. I
know what it's like because I lived that way until I was twenty-one
years old . . . Tell her, Kate, what it is to be an older sister. To suddenly be the one who has to work and shoulder all the responsibilities
and not be the one who gets the affection and the hugs when you
were the only one there. You think I don't see it with Stanley and
Eugene! With Nora and Laurie? You think I don't hear the fights that
go on up in those rooms night after night. Go on, Kate! Scream at
her! Yell at her. Call her names, Blanche. Tell her to go to hell for
the first time in your life . . . And when you both got it out of your
systems, give each other a hug and go have dinner. My lousy ice
cream is melting, for God's sake. (*There is a long silence.*)

Nora. ACT II.

*Nora is still smarting over Blanche's decision not to allow her to
participate in a Broadway production. She is disrespectful, bitchy,*

and judgmental. When Blanche angrily tells her that Nora has no right to judge her, Nora lashes out, exploding in an outburst of deep-seated feelings.

NORA

Judge you? I can't even talk to you. I don't exist to you. I have tried so hard to get close to you but there was never any room. Whatever you had to give went to Daddy, and when he died, whatever was left you gave to—(*She turns away.*)

Intervening speech. Blanche: What? Finish what you were going to say.

NORA (*cont'd.*)

. . . I have been jealous my whole life of Laurie because she was lucky enough to be born sick. I could never turn a light on in my room at night or read in bed because Laurie always needed her precious sleep. I could never have a friend over on the weekends because Laurie was always resting. I used to pray I'd get some terrible disease or get hit by a car so I'd have a leg all twisted or crippled and then once, maybe just once, *I'd* get to crawl in bed next to you on a cold rainy night and talk to you and hold you until I fell asleep in your arms . . . just once . . . (*She is in tears.*)

Blanche. ACT II.

Blanche responds to Nora's outburst above. Showing grit and determination, she commits herself to a future without self-recrimination and self-pity.

BLANCHE

(*Hesitates, trying to recover.*) . . . I'm not going to let you hurt me, Nora. I'm not going to let you tell me that I don't love you or that I haven't tried to give you as much as I gave Laurie . . . God knows I'm not perfect because enough angry people in this house told me so tonight . . . But I am *not* going to be a doormat for all the frustrations and unhappiness that you or Aunt Kate or anyone else wants to lay at my feet . . . I did *not* create this universe. I do *not* decide who lives and dies, or who's rich or poor or who feels loved and who feels deprived. If you feel cheated that Laurie gets more than you, then I feel cheated that I had a husband who died at thirty-six. And if you keep on feeling that way, you'll end up like me . . . with something much worse than loneliness or helplessness and that's self-pity. Believe me, there is no leg that's twisted or bent that is more crippling than a human being who thrives on his own misfortunes . . . I am sorry, Nora, that you feel unloved and I will do everything I can to change it except apologize for it. I am tired of apologizing. After a while it becomes your life's work and it doesn't bring any money into the house . . . If it's taken your pain and Aunt Kate's anger to get me to start living again, then God will give me strength to make it up to you, but I will *not* go back to being that frightened, helpless woman that I created! . . . I've already buried someone I love. Now it's time to bury someone I hate.

BILOXI BLUES
(V L)

Premièred March 28, 1985
at the Neil Simon Theatre, New York City

CAST

Roy Selridge	Brian Tarantina
Joseph Wykowski	Matt Mulhern
Don Carney	Alan Ruck
Eugene Morris Jerome	Matthew Broderick
Arnold Epstein	Barry Miller
Sgt. Merwin J. Toomey	Bill Sadler
James Hennesey	Goeffrey Sharp
Rowena	Randall Edwards
Daisy Hannigan	Penelope Ann Miller

All set pieces are representational, stylized, and free-flowing. It is 1943.

The plot of the play is propelled by the narrative of Eugene Morris Jerome, a young draftee and aspiring writer from Brighton Beach, New York who wants to achieve three things while in the service: lose his virginity, fall in love, and become a writer. Eugene and his buddies, a motley group, have been in the Army just four days before arriving for basic training at Biloxi, Mississippi where they are greeted by Sergeant Merwin J. Toomey a profane, battle-hardened disciplinarian. Toomey sadistically upbraids the boys and takes an instant dislike to Arnold Epstein, an intelligent, sensitive fellow who is as strong-willed in his beliefs as Toomey is in his. This sets up a battle of attrition between the two, during which Epstein is subjected to interminable latrine duty, racial slurs, and humiliating derision from Toomey as well as his buddies. But Epstein maintains his dignity in a wonderful example of strength of character.

While on a twenty-four-hour pass Eugene attains one of his goals—he loses his virginity to a prostitute. Back at the base, things heat up when one of the platoon is arrested for committing a homosexual act. He is identified and is carted off for punishment by Sergeant Toomey.

On the eve of his going to the veterans hospital, a drunken Toomey confronts Epstein with a loaded .45 and forces Epstein to arrest him for the crime of threatening an enlisted man while intoxicated. This is a ploy to trick Epstein into becoming an obedient, disciplined soldier. Epstein reluctantly obeys, sentencing Toomey to a hundred push-ups. The next day Toomey leaves, never to return.

Before shipping out, Eugene visits Daisy Hannigan, a nice Catholic girl he had met at the U.S.O. They express their love for each other and seal their feelings with a kiss. Eugene has accomplished his second goal—he has fallen in love.

Overseas, Eugene's buddies are disbursed to the battlefields of Europe (their fate is described in the curtain monologue at the end of this section). But Eugene is injured in a Jeep accident in England and never sees active duty. Instead he is given an assignment as a writer for *Stars and Stripes*, resulting in him achieving his final goal—he has become a writer.

Toomey. ACT I.

Eugene and his buddies have just arrived at boot camp in Biloxi, Mississippi, and have been called to attention by their Sergeant, Merwin J. Toomey, a battle-hardened disciplinarian.

TOOMEY

(*To the Men.*) . . . My name is Toomey. Sergeant Merwin J. Toomey and I am in charge of C Company during your ten weeks of basic training here in Beautiful Biloxi, Mississippi, after which those of you who have survived the heat, humidity, roaches, spiders, snakes, dry rot, fungus, dysentery, syphilis, gonorrhea and tick fever, will be sent to some shit island in the Paicific or some turd pile in Northern Sicily. In either case, returning to your mommas and poppas with your balls intact is highly improbable. There's only one way to come out of a war healthy of body and sane of mind and that way is to be born the favorite daughter of the President of the United States . . . I speak from experience having served fourteen months in the North African campaign where seventy-three percent of my comrades are buried under the sand of the A-rab desert. The colorful ribbons on my chest will testify to the fact that my government is greatful for my contribution having donated a small portion of my brains to this confilct, the other portion being protected by a heavy steel plate in my head. This injury has caused me to become a smart, compassionate, understanding and sympathetic teacher of raw, young men—or the cruelest, craziest, most sadistic Goddamn son of a bitch you ever saw. . . and that's something you won't know until ten weeks from now, do I make myself clear, Epstein?

Toomey. ACT I.

Toomey, in a sadistic display of authority, has ordered the men to the floor to do one hundred push-ups. Everyone except Eugene, that is, whom Toomey has spared as a means of turning the others against him.

TOOMEY

Now we are moving ahead in our quest for discipline . . . As the sweat pours off your brows and your puny muscles strain to lift your flabby, chubby, jellied bodies, think of Private Jerome of Brighton Beach, New York, who is *not* down there beside you. *Not* sharing your pain, *not* sharing your struggle . . . Fate always chooses someone to get a free ride. The kind of man who always gets away with all kinds of shit. In this company it seems to be Private Eugene M. Jerome. Eventually we get to hate those men. Hate them, loathe them and despise them. How does Private Jerome learn to deal with this cold wall of anger and hostility? By learning to endure it alone. That, gentlemen, is the supreme lesson in discipline. You're slowing down, boys. The sooner you finish, the sooner you'll get to our fine Southern cooking . . . Up down . . . Up down . . . Carry on instructions, Jerome. Up down . . . Up down . . . (*Toomey leaves.*)

Arnold. ACT I.

Arnold Epstein is frail, sensitive, and intelligent—making him a terrible candidate for the U.S. Army. He is also a boldly out-spoken critic of Army life and, therefore, a catalyst for the sadistic temperament of Sergeant Toomey. For refusing to eat the slop they serve in the mess, Arnold has just completed five days of K.P., including cleaning up the latrines. Here he tells Eugene of the humiliation he has suffered at the hands of brutal ingrates.

ARNOLD

. . . I was in the latrine alone. I spent four hours cleaning it, on my hands and knees. It looked better than my mother's bathroom at home. Then these two non-coms come in, one was the cook, that three-hundred-pound guy and some other slob, with cigar butts in their mouths and reeking from beer . . . They come in to pee only instead of using the urinal, they use one of the johns, both peeing in the same one, making circles, figure-eights. Then they start to walk out and I say, "Hey, I just cleaned that. Please flush the johns." And the big one, the cook, says to me, "Up your ass, rookie," or some other really clever remark . . . And I block the doorway and I say, "There's a printed order on the wall signed by Captain Landon stating the regulations that all facilities must be flushed after using" . . . And I'm requesting that they follow regulations, since I was left in charge, and to please flush the facility . . . And the big one says to me, "Suppose you flush it, New York Jew Kike." and I said my ethnic heritage notwithstanding, please flush the facility . . . They look at each other, this half a ton of brainless beef and suddenly rush me, turn me upside down, grab my an-kles and—and—and they lowered me by my feet with my head in the toilet, in their filth, their poison . . . all the way until I couldn't breathe . . . then they pulled off my belt and tied my feet onto the ceiling pipes with my head still in their foul waste and tied my hands behind my back with dirty rags, and they left me there, hanging like a pig that was going to be slaughtered . . . I wasn't strong enough to fight back. I couldn't do it alone. No one came to help me . . . Then the pipe broke and I fell to the ground . . . It took me twenty minutes to get myself untied . . . Twenty minutes! But it will take me the rest of my life to wash off my humiliation. I was degraded. I lost my dignity. If I stay, Gene, if they put a gun in my hands, one night, I swear to God, I'll kill them both . . . I'm not a murderer. I don't want to disgrace my family . . . But I have to get out of here . . . Now do you understand?

Toomey. ACT I.

The men are preparing to leave the base on a forty-eight-hour pass when Wykowski announces that someone has stolen sixty-two dollars from his wallet. As a means of uncovering the perpetrator, Toomey lines the men up and demands that the thief step forward with the money. There will be no forty-eight hours of well-deserved freedom until the money is recovered.

Although he is not the thief (Toomey has taken the sixty-two dollars as a lesson to those who leave money about carelessly), Epstein steps forward and places the money on the locker. He is willing to take the blame so that the others may be issued passes. But Toomey, in a fit of twisted logic, finds his act of benevolence abhorrent and confines him to quarters.

TOOMEY

(*Calmly.*) Gentlemen, I think we have a problem. All those wishing to help me solve it, get your asses in here before the firing squad leaves for the weekend. ON THE DOUBLE! Ten-hut! (*The lights go up on the barracks area, off on latrine. All six soldiers rush in and line up at attention in front of their bunks. Toomey, dressed for weekend leave, walks slowly in front of them, thinking very sreriously.*) I have been in this man's army now for twelve years, four months and twenty-three days and during my tenure as a noncommissioned officer, I have put up with everything from mutiny to sodomy. I consider mutiny and sodomy relatively minor offenses. Mutiny is an act of aggression due to a rising expression of unreleased repressed feelings. Sodomy is the result of doing something you don't want to do with someone you don't want to do it with because of no access to do what you want to do with someone you can't get to do it with.

Intervening speech. Eugene: (*To audience.*) It makes sense if you think it out slowly.

TOOMEY (*cont'd.*)

Burglary, on the other hand, is a cheapshit crime. And I frown on that. In the past thirty-one days, you boys have made some fine progress. You're not fighting soldiers yet, but I'd match you up against some Nazi cocktail waitress any time. That's why it was my recommendation that this platoon receive a forty-eight-hour pass . . . But until we clear up the mystery of Private Wykowski's missing sixty-two dollars, there will be no forty-eight hour passes issued until you are old and gray soldiers of World War II, marching as American Legionnaires in the Armistice Day Parade. I am asking the guilty party to place sixty-two dollars on this here foot-locker within the next thirty seconds . . . I offer no leniency, no forgiveness and no abstention from punishment. What I do offer is honor and integrity, and the respect of his fellow soldiers, knowing that it was *his* act of courage that enabled them to enjoy the brief freedom they so richly deserve. (*He looks at his watch.*) I am counting down to thirty . . . It is of this time that heroes are made . . . One . . . two . . . three . . . four . . . five . . . (*They all look at each other silently.*) . . . six seven . . . eight . . .

Arnold. ACT II.

In his absence, Wykowski has taken Eugene's notebook of memoirs from his locker and is reading its contents to the others. When Eugene returns to find his notes missing, Wykowski callously continues to read them aloud while Eugene is restrained by Selridge. When Eugene is released, he reaches for his book, but it is snatched from his grasp by Arnold, who reads aloud about himself after Eugene's leaves.

ARNOLD

Sure, Kowski. This is what we're fighting the war about, isn't it? (*He reads.*) "Arnold Epstein is truly the most complex and fascinating man I've ever met and his constant and relentless pursuit of truth, logic and reason fascinates me in the same proportion as his obstinacy and unnecessary heroics drive me to distraction. But I love him for it. In the same manner that I love Joe DiMaggio for making the gesture of catching a long fly ball to center seem like the last miracle performed by God in modern times. But often I hold back showing my love and affection for Arnold because I think he might misinterpret it. It just happens to be my instinctive feeling—that Arnold is homo-sexual, and it bothers me that it bothers me." (*He closes the books. He looks at the others who are all staring at him.*) . . . Do you see why I find life so interesting? Here is a man of my own faith and background, potentially intelligent and talented, who in six weeks has come to the brilliant conclusion that a cretin like Wykowski is going to win the Medal of Honor and that I, his most esteemed and dearest friend, is a fairy. (*He tosses the book on Eugene's bunk.*) This is a problem worthy of a Talmudic scholar. Good-night, fellas . . . It is my opinion that no one gets a wink of sleep tonight.

Toomey. ACT II.

Toomey has awakened the men to inform them that one among them is suspected of committing a homosexual act.

TOOMEY

UP! Everybody UP! Goddammit! It is two-fifteen in the morning and I've got a headache, a problem and a God damn temper all at the same time. Move your asses, we've got some serious talking to do. MOVE IT! (*He bangs the bedpost again. They all get out of bed,*

mumbling their surprise and indignation. All stand at attention be-
side their bunks. Toomey paces back and forth, silently and angrily.)
. . . Is there any among you who does not know the meaning of the
word, fellatio? (*Some of them look at each other.*) For the uninformed, fellatio is the act of committing oral intercourse . . . Is there
any among you who does not know the meaning of the word "oral"
or "intercourse"? . . . It is encouraging to know that my platoon is
made up of mental giants . . . At exactly 0155 this morning, Sergeant
Riley of Baker Company entered the darkened latrine situated in his
barracks . . . When he hit the light switch, lo and behold, he encoun-
tered two members of this regiment in the act of the aforementioned
exercise . . . When I was in the Boy Scouts, that kind of thing came
under the heading of "experimentation" . . . In the wartime U.S.
Army, it is considered a criminal offense, punishable by court-mar-
tial, dishonorable discharge and a possible five-year prison term . . .
The soldier in Company B was a—(*Looks at clipboard.*) Private
Harvey J. Lindstrom. The other soldier, whose back was to Sergeant
Riley, was not seen and made his escape by jumping out an open
window with his pants somewhere around his ankles, a feat of dex-
terity worthy of a paratrooper . . . Sergeant Riley, a man with five
rounds of shrapnel in his right leg, gave chase to no avail but re-
ported seeing the man enter this barracks at approximately oh two
hundred hours . . . These are the facts, gentlemen. I will be brief.
Does the guilty party wish to step forward, admit his indiscretion and
save this company, what I promise you, will be pain, anguish and
humiliation beyond the endurance of man? (*No one moves.*) No, I
didn't think so . . . I'm just going to have to pick him out, won't
I? . . . It's amazing what you can find out when you go eyeball to
eyeball . . . (*He crosses to Wykowski and indeed goes eyeball to eyeball. He moves on and does it with all six men.*) Don't blink, Selridge
. . . Look at me . . . Stand up, soldier . . . (*No one breathes. No one
bats an eye.*) There were two eyeballs in there whose shoes I

wouldn't want to be in . . . Private Lindstrom will be interrogated in the morning. If he names the man he consorted with tonight, it is very possible Private Lindstrom's sentence will be significantly lessened. A worrisome thought to the gentleman whose eyeballs I just referred to . . . In the meantime all privileges on base are canceled, all weekend leaves are likewise canceled . . . The moral of this story is—when you get real horny, do unto yourself what you would otherwise do unto others . . . (*He turns and leaves. The others breathe at last and finally look at each other.*)

Eugene. ACT II.

In this curtain speech, Eugene summarizes post-Biloxi events.

EUGENE

So far, two of my main objectives came true . . . I lost my virginity and I fell in love. Now all I had to do was become a writer and stay alive . . . On that first train ride to Biloxi, we were all nervous . . . On the train now heading for an Atlantic seaport, we were all scared . . . I closed my notebook and tried to sleep . . . (*He closes notebook.*) . . . When I opened the notebook two years later, I was on a train just like this one, heading for Fort Dix, New Jersey, to be discharged . . . I reread what I wrote to see how accurate my predictions were the night Wykowski broke into my locker . . . Roy Selridge served in every campaign in France, was eventually made a sergeant and sent back to Biloxi to train new recruits. He has men doing three hundred push-ups a day . . . Wykowski was wounded at Arnheim by a mortar shell. He lost his right leg straight up to the hip. He didn't get the Medal of Honor, but he was cited for outstanding courage in battle . . . Don Carney, after six months of constant attack by enemy fire, was hospitalized for severe depression and neurological disorders. He never sings anymore . . . Arnold Epstein was listed as missing in action and his body was never traced or found. But Arnold's a tricky guy. He might still be alive teaching philosophy in Greece somewhere. He just never liked doing things the Army way. . . . Daisy Hannigan married a doctor from New Orleans. Her name is now Daisy Horowitz. Oh, well . . . She sends me a postcard every time she has a new baby . . . As for me, I never saw a day's action. I was in a Jeep accident my first day in England and my back was so badly injured, they wanted to send me home. Instead they gave me a job writing for *Stars and Stripes*, the G.I. newspaper. I still suffer pangs of guilt because my career was enhanced by World War II . . . I'll tell you one thing, I'm glad I didn't know all that the night our train left Biloxi for places and events unknown! (*Carney begins singing a whimsical, romantic song of the period as . . .*)

THE CURTAIN FALLS

BROADWAY BOUND

Premièred December 4, 1986
at the Broadhurst Theatre, New York City

Directed by Gene Saks

CAST

Kate	Linda Lavin
Ben	John Randolph
Eugene	Jonathan Silverman
Stan	Jason Alexander
Blanche	Phyllis Newman
Jack	Philip Sterling

The action of the play takes place in a house in Brighton Beach, Brooklyn, New York.

The Jeromes' Brighton Beach home is inhabited by Kate and Jack, their sons Eugene and Stan, and Kate's father, Ben. Kate is a practical homemaker, Jack is a cutter in the garment district, Eugene and Stan are aspiring comedy writers, and Ben is a cranky old Socialist who refuses to live with his wife in his granddaughter Blanche's Park Avenue apartment.

While Kate is plain and lives humbly, Blanche is pretty and wealthy and carries guilt feelings as a consequence. And her pleas with Ben to reconcile with his wife and move to Florida result in her being hurt by his cold irascibility and lack of affection.

The thirty-three-year-old marriage between Kate and Jack is strained because Kate is harboring the fact that she knows Jack had been intimate with another woman. But she has said nothing, hoping that the affair would prove transitory. But when she discovers that Jack has renewed the relationship, she can no longer remain silent and confronts him with the facts. Jack reluctantly admits to the affair. But his confession is self-satisfying. Kate is hurt and left with feelings of inadequacy and anger. Their domestic relationship degenerates into one of either referring to each other in the third person or not speaking. In the meantime, Eugene and Stan have gotten an assignment writing for a new comedy show on CBS radio. They are elated, but their elation is short-lived when Jack interprets their humor as a direct reflection upon family and friends and, more specifically, upon his act of infidelity. The boys try to reason with Jack, but his guilt renders him irrational, and when he attempts to defend his mistress, Stan stands up for his mother in a noble but relationship-fracturing outburst.

Jack moves out of the house, and when Eugene and Stan score as writers for Phil Silvers, they decide to move to New York City. They have outgrown Brighton Beach and it is time to move on. Jack eventually remarries, Ben finally succumbs to the sunny beaches of Miami, and Kate remains in her home, basking in the glory of her sons' success.

Jack. ACT I.

After thirty-three years, the marriage of Kate and Jack Jerome has become sub-Platonic. Jack is listless, uncommunicative, and no longer affectionate. Kate, suspecting infidelity, has confronted Jack with this proposition. After an embarrassing interlude of denial, Jack finally opens up regarding his feelings and admits to having had an affair.

JACK

I've stopped feeling for everything. Getting up in the morning, going to bed at night . . . Why do I do it? Maybe it was the war. The war came along and after that, nothing was the same. I hated poverty, but I knew how to deal with it. I don't know my place anymore. When I was a boy in temple, I looked at the old men and thought, "They're so wise. They must know all the secrets of the world." . . . I'm a middle-aged man and I don't know a damned thing. Wisdom doesn't come with age. It comes with wisdom . . . I'm not wise, and I never will be . . . I don't even lie very well . . . There was a woman. (*Kate stares at him.*) About a year ago. I met her in a restaurant on Seventh Avenue. She worked in a bank, a widow. Not all that attractive, but refined woman, spoke very well, better educated than I was . . . It was a year ago, Kate. It didn't last long. I never thought it would . . . and it's over now. If I've hurt you, and God knows you have every right to be, then I apologize. I'm sorry. But I'll be truthful with you. I didn't tell it to you just now out of a great sense of honesty. I told you because I couldn't carry the weight of all that guilt on my back anymore. (*Jack waits quietly for her reaction.*)

Jack. ACT I.

After Jack admits to an affair, Kate probes him regarding the other woman. He pleads with her not to do so. But she is understandably hurt and angry and is adamant that he tell her why he chose this woman in particular. Jack reluctantly does so.

JACK

This is a mistake, Kate. A mistake we'll both regret, as God is my judge . . . Why this woman? Because she had an interest in life besides working in a bank or taking care of her house. To her, the world was bigger than that. She read books I never heard of, talked about places I never knew existed. When she talked, I just listened. And when *I* talked, I suddenly heard myself say things I never knew I felt. Because she asked questions that I had to answer . . . Learning about yourself can be a very dangerous thing, Kate. Some people, like me, should leave well enough alone . . . The things you were afraid to hear, I won't tell you, because they're true. It lasted less time than you think, but once was enough to hurt, I realize that . . . I never ate in that restaurant again, and I have never once seen her again . . . if either one of us feels better now that I've told you all that, then shame on both of us. (*Jack sits at the table, opposite Kate. She turns away from him.*) If I killed a man on the street, you would probably stand by me. Maybe even understand it. So why is this the greatest sin that can happen to a man and wife?

Kate. ACT I.

Jack's revelations have been truly hurtful. He has not only broken the trust between them, he has also made Kate feel unappreciated and intellectually inadequate. When he asks her what she wants to do, this is her response:

KATE

What do *I* want to do? Is that how it works? You have an affair, and I get the choice of forgetting about it or living alone for the rest of my life? . . . It's so simple for you, isn't it? I am so angry. I am so hurt by your selfishness. You break what was good between us and leave me to pick up the pieces . . . and *still* you continue to lie to me.

Intervening speech. Jack: I told you everything.

KATE (*cont'd.*)

(*Sitting in US dining chair.*) I knew about that woman a year ago. I got a phone call from a friend. I won't even tell you who . . . "What's going on with you and Jack?" she asks me. "Are you two still together? Who's this woman he's having lunch with every day?" she asks me . . . I said, "Did you see them together?" . . . She said, "No, but I heard." . . . I said, "Don't believe what you hear. Believe what you see!" and I hung up on her . . . Did I do good, Jack? Did I defend my husband like a good wife? . . . A year I lived with that, hoping to God it wasn't true and if it was, praying it would go away . . . And God was good to me. No more phone calls, no more stories about Jack and his lunch partner . . . No more wondering why you were coming home late from work even when it wasn't busy season . . . Until this morning. Guess wo calls me? . . . Guess who Jack was having lunch with in the same restaurant twice last week? . . . Last year's lies don't hold up this year, Jack . . . This year you have to deal with it. (*Jack looks at her, remains silent for a moment.*)

Stan. ACT II.

A month has passed, and the tension between Kate and Jack is evident. They are not speaking and are addressing each other in the third person. But their sons, Eugene and Stan, are elated because they have landed a job writing for a new show on CBS radio.

After the show airs, Jack is upset because he draws parallels between what the boys have written and the neighborhood and his household, and, out of underlying guilt, is particularly sensitive about dialogue that he feels called attention to his affair. The boys deny pernicious intent, but Jack is relentless, triggering a hostile exchange between him and Stan. And when Jack attempts to defend the reputation of the woman with whom he is having an affair, Stan is courageous in defense of his mother.

STAN

(*Standing.*) I don't care if she's Joan of Arc, that's still my mother we're talking about. Do whatever you God damn please, but don't blame Gene and me of humiliating you when you're the one who's been humiliating *us* . . . You're so damn guilty for what you've done, you're accusing everyone else of betraying *you* . . . I never wanted to hear what was happening to you and Mom. I prayed every night you would both work it out and it would pass out of our lives. You could have called each other "him" and "her" forever as long as it kept you together . . . All my life you taught me about things like dignity and principles and I believed them. I still do, I guess . . . But what kind of principles does a man have when he tells his sons the woman's he's seeing on the side is a wonderful, decent human being?

Kate. ACT II.

Later the same evening, while Kate and Eugene are alone, she speaks fondly of the old days, her grandparents, expresses her belief in the importance of family tradition. Eugene loves his mother and her stories and insists that she repeat the one about the time she danced with George Raft.

At the conclusion of her story, Eugene and Kate dance together in a touching moment between mother and son.

Preceding speech. Eugene: Did you have a—you know—a crush on him?

KATE

On George Raft? You think I'm crazy? He was Italian. I was in enough trouble already. He wasn't my type anyway . . . Your father was the one I had the crush on . . . Since I was thirteen years old. He was five years older then me. He went with a whole other crowd. In those days young people didn't tell each other they had crushes on them. You had to guess. So you sent messages with your eyes, your face, the way you walked by them.

Intervening speech. Eugene: How did you walk by him?

KATE (*cont'd.*)

Not too much, not too little. But he was hard to figure out. He was never a show-off, never a fancy Dan. He didn't smile a lot, but when he did, you knew he meant it. Most boys then smiled at everything. They thought it gave them a good personality. Jack was too honest to put on a good personality. He was what he was . . . and to get a smile from Jack Jerome, you knew you had to earn it . . . But it cost him plenty. The smilers got to be the salesmen. The smilers got to be the bosses. The smilers got all the girls. Your father paid the price for not being a phony . . . It was hard to impress him. That's why I went to the Primrose that night. I thought if Jack heard that I danced with George Raft, maybe I'd get him to notice me.

Intervening speech. Eugene: This is a movie. There's a whole movie in this story, Ma. And one day I'm going to write it.

KATE (*cont'd.*)

So that night, in a pouring rain, me and Adele Abrams went to the Primrose. My hair got soaking wet, I lost my curls, I wanted to die. But then I got this brilliant idea. Instead of drying it, I combed it straight down and left it wet. Jet black hair. I looked like a Latin from Manhattan . . . The perfect partner for George Raft . . . When I walked out of the ladies' room, my own friends didn't recognize me.

Intervening speech. Eugene: I can't believe this is *my mother* you're talking about.

KATE (*cont'd.*)

Don't worry. I knew God was going to punish me for the wet hair, too . . . Ten boys must have asked me to dance. But I said no to all of them because I didn't want to tire myself out . . . And then I started to get scared. Because it was ten after eleven and he still didn't show up. If I wasn't home by twelve, my parents would walk in and find out I was lying to them. And with my mother, I didn't need God to punish me.

Intervening speech. Eugene: Twelve o'clock! Cinderella! This story has everything.

KATE (*cont'd.*)

And then, at twenty after eleven, he walks in . . . Like the King of Spain. My heart was beating louder than the drummer in the band . . . He had two friends with him, one on each side, like bodyguards. And I swear, there was something in their inside pockets. I thought to myself, they're either guns or more jars of grease for his hair.

Intervening speech. Eugene: (*To audience*.) She actually had a sense of humor. This was a side of my mother I hardly ever saw. (*To Kate*.) So, he walks in with these two guys.

KATE (*cont'd.*)
(*Taking off her sweater and standing C*.) So, he walks in with these two friends and I know I don't have much time. So I grabbed Bobby Zugetti, a shoe clerk, who was the best dancer at the Primrose, and said, "Bobby, dance with me!" . . . I knew he had a crush on me and I never gave him a tumble before. He didn't know what hit him. So out on the floor we go, and we fox-trotted from one side of the ballroom and back. In and out, bobbing and weaving through the crowd, gliding across the floor like a pair of ice skaters.

Intervening speech. Eugene: "Begin the Beguine" . . . Maybe "Night and Day." That's what I would use in the picture.

KATE (*cont'd.*)
And I never once looked over to see if George Raft was looking at me . . . I wanted to get *his* attention, I didn't want to give him mine . . . The music finishes and Bobby dips me down to the floor. It was a little lower than a nice girl should dip, but I figured one more sin wouldn't kill me . . . And I walk over to Adele, I'm dripping with perspiration, and I said, "Well? Did he watch me?" . . . And she said, "It's hard to tell. His eyes don't move." So I look over and he's sitting at a table with his two friends and Adele is right. His eyes don't move. And it's twenty-five to twelve, and he's never even noticed me. And I said to myself, "Well, if it's not meant to be, it's not meant to be." . . . And Adele and I started for the door.

Intervening speech. Eugene: The tension mounts. The audience is on the edge of their seats.

KATE (*cont'd.*)

As we pass their table, George Raft stands up and says, "Excuse me."
And he's looking right at Adele Abrams. He says, "Could I ask you a
question, please?" Adele is shaking like a leaf. And she walks over to
him.

Intervening speech. Eugene: Adele? He's talking to Adele Abrams?

KATE (*cont'd.*)

And he says, "I wonder if your friend would care to dance with me?"
. . . And she says, "You want *me* to ask her?" . . . And he says,
"Please. I'm a little shy."

Intervening speech. Eugene: I don't believe it. I don't believe George Raft
said that.

KATE (*Cont'd.*)

I swear to God. May I never live to see another day.

Intervening speech. Eugene: Even if it's true, it's out of the picture. An
audience would never believe it.

KATE (*cont'd.*)

Fine. So Adele says, "I'll ask her." . . . So she comes back and asks
me . . . And I look at him and he smiles at me . . . And his eyes
moved for the first time. Not fresh or anything, but he had the look of
a man with a lot of confidence and I never saw that before. Scared
the life out of me. So I walk over to him and he takes my hand and
leads me out to the floor . . . Everyone in the Primrose is watching.
Even the band. Someone had to whisper, "Start playing," so they
would begin . . . And they began. And we danced around that room.
And I held my head high and my back straight as a board . . . And I

looked down at the floor and up at the ceiling, but never in his eyes. I saw a professional do that once . . . His hands were so gentle. Hardly touching me at all, but I knew exactly when he wanted me to move and which way he wanted me to turn.

Eugene. ACT II.

Jack has moved out, leaving Kate with her father and the boys whose careers are on the upswing. And when they are hired to write for the "Phil Silvers Show", Stan announces that it is time for them to leave Brighton Beach for their own apartment in New York City.

It is the day of their departure, and Stan has run ahead in search of a taxi to take them to their new digs. But Eugene, in a nostalgic mood, stays behind for a moment to look at their home. In this speech which ends the play, he speaks of matters past, present and future.

EUGENE

(*Speaking to the audience.*) I knew then that no matter how many times I came back to see this house, it would never be my home again . . . Mom and Pop split up for good and never got back together . . . As a matter-of-fact, he remarried about two years later to a pretty nice woman. Mom would really be hurt if she heard me say that, but the truth is the truth . . . Grandpa found it rough going in his seventy-eighth year and finally surrendered to Capitalism and Miami Beach . . . He plays pinochle every day and donates half his winnings to the Socialist Party . . . Josie and I got married and we sleep each night with her hand lying gently across my chest. I won't even breathe for fear she'll move it away.

Intervening speech. Stan: (*Running down the street to Eugene.*) Gene! Come on! I got a cab!

Intervening speech. Eugene: I'm coming. I'm coming.

Intervening speech. Stan: I never realized how cold it was out here before. (*Stan exits up the street, taking Eugene's box of cookies with him.*)

EUGENE (*cont'd.*)

I didn't keep my promise to Pop. I opened his letter and read it. He didn't apologize, and he wasn't mad at Stan and me for what we wrote. The only thing he wanted was for Stan and me to understand his side of the story . . . Only he never said what his side was . . . Contrary to popular belief, everything in life doesn't come to a clear-cut conclusion. Mom didn't do anything very exciting with the rest of her life except wax her grandmother's table and bask in the joy of her sons' success. But I never got the feeling that Mom felt she sacrificed herself for us. Whatever she gave, she found her own quiet pleasure in. I guess she was never comfortable with words like "I love you." A hard life can sometimes knock the sentiment out of you . . . But all in all, she considers herself a pretty lucky woman. After all, she did one dance with George Raft. (*Eugene turns away from the house, grabs his suitcase and runs up the street to the cab.*)

RUMORS

Premièred September 22, 1988
at the Old Globe Theatre, San Diego, California

Directed by Gene Saks

CAST

Chris Gorman	Christine Baranski
Ken Gorman	Mark Nelson
Claire Ganz	Jessica Walter
Lenny Ganz	Ron Leibman
Ernie Cusack	Andre Gregory
Cookie Cusack	Joyce Van Patten
Glenn Cooper	Ken Howard
Cassie Cooper	Lisa Banes
Officer Welch	Charles Brown
Officer Pudney	Cynthia Darlow

The action of the play takes place in an old Victorian house in Sneden's Landing, New York.

On the eve of Charley and Myra Brock's tenth wedding anniversary, Ken and Chris Gorman arrive to the sound of a gunshot and find Charley in his bedroom with a superficially wounded ear lobe. And wife Myra is missing. Not fully aware of the facts, but wishing to cover up potential scandal, Ken and Chris hastily contrive to obfuscate the possiblity of attempted suicide. As the other party guests arrive, they are drawn into the cover-up, and, in the tradition of true farce, the evening becomes a hilarious tangle of word-play, double entendre, and mistaken identity escalating to a fanciful climax speech by Ken Gorman posing as Charley Brock.

Welch. ACT II.

The party guests think that the officers have come as a result of gun-shots and, out of panic and fear of implication, they offer outra-geously implausible explanations. But Officer Welch and Pudney have come to merely investigate the circumstances of an auto acci-dent. But when a slip-of-the-tongue and a police radio report indi-cate that gunshots have come from the property, Officer Welch be-comes impatient with the ridiculous babble and apparent stalling.

WELCH

You and everybody else, m'am. I'm going to say something now that is not really a part of my official capacity. But I don't believe one God damn thing I've heard in this room. I think there were gunshots here tonight. I think someone or *everyone* is trying to cover up something. A man gets hit in the nose, another man stabs himself with a fork, someone's BMW gets smashed up, the host takes a short-legged dog for a walk and then goes to sleep, the hostess takes her father to a hospital in California with a broken hip, and nobody hears two gunshots because because everybody is dancing, including a woman named Cookie who's been cooking all night who can't stand or walk! You people have to deal with me. I'm a real cop, you understand? I'm not somebody named Elmer that your kids watch on the Disney Channel . . . Now, I want some *real* answers, intelligent answers, believable answers, and answers that don't make me laugh. But first, I want to see Mr. Charley Brock and find out what the hell's going on here—including the possibility of him having two bullet holes in him. Now, I'll give you five seconds to get him down here, or I'll take two seconds and go upstairs and find him.

Lenny. ACT II.

*Lenny, posing as Charley Brock, offers the following fanciful expla-
nation to Officer Welch for the events of the evening. He begins the
highly contrived tale with trepidation but, once into the fabrication,
gains confidence and delivers the monologue with flair and confidence. (As a crowning irony, there may be more truth to his story
than he imagined.)*

LENNY

Okay . . . Let's see . . . the story . . . as it happened . . . as I remember
it . . . as I'm telling it . . . oh, God! . . . Well, here goes . . . At exactly
six o'clock tonight I came home from work. My wife, Myra, was in
her dressing room getting dressed for the party. I got a bottle of
champagne from the refrigerator and headed upstairs. Rosita, the
Spanish cook, was in the kitchen with Ramona, her Spanish sister
and Romero, her Spanish son. They were preparing an Italian dinner.
They were waiting for Myra to tell her when to start the dinner. As I
climbed the stairs, I said to myself, "It's my tenth wedding anniversary and I can't believe I still love my wife so much." Myra was
putting on the perfume I bought her for Christmas. I purposely buy it
because it drives me crazy . . . I tapped on her door. Tap tap tap. She
opens it. I hand her a glass of champagne. I make a toast. (*Looking at
Claire.*) "To the most beautiful wife a man ever had for ten years."
She says, "To the best man and the best ten years a beautiful wife
ever had" . . . We drink. We kiss. We toast again. "To the loveliest
skin on the loveliest body that has never aged a day in ten wonderful
years" . . . She toasts, "To the gentlest hands that ever stroked the
loveliest skin that never has aged in ten wonderful years" . . . We
drink. We kiss. We toast . . . We drink. We kiss. We toast . . . By
seven o'clock the bottle is finished, my wife is sloshed and I'm
completely toasted . . . And then I smell the perfume. The perfume I

could never resist . . . I loved her in that moment with as much passion and ardor as the night we were first newlyweds. (*Rising. To
Welch.*) I tell you this, not with embarrassment, but with pride and
joy for a love that grows stronger and more lasting as each new day
passes. We lay there spent, naked in each other's arms, complete in
our happiness. It's now eight o'clock and outside it's grown dark.
Suddenly, a gentle knock on the door. Knock knock knock. The door
opens and a strange young man looks down at us with a knife in his
hands. Myra screams. (*He begins to act out the story.*) I jump up and
run for the gun in my drawer. Myra grabs a towel and shields herself.
I rush back in with the pistol, ready to save my wife's life. The
strange young man says in Spanish, Yo quito se dablo enchilada por
quesa in quinto minuto." But I don't speak Spanish and I never saw
Rosita's son, Romero, before, and I didn't know the knife was to cut
up the salad and he was asking should they heat up the dinner now?
So I aimed my gun at him, Myra screams and pulls my arm. The gun
goes off and shoots me in the ear lobe. Rosita's son, Romero, runs
downstairs and tells Rosita and Romona, "Mamasetta! Meela que
paso el hombre ay baco ay yah. El hombre que loco, que bang-
bang."—the crazy man took a shot at him. So, Rosita, Ramona and
Romero leave in a huff. My ear lobe is bleeding all over Myra's new
dress. Suddenly we hear a car pull up. It's the first guests. Myra
grabs a bathrobe and runs downstairs to stop Rosita, Ramona, and
Romero, otherwise we'll have no dinner. But they drive off in their
Alfa Romeo. I look out the window, but it's dark and I think someone is stealing my beautiful old Mercedes, so I take another shot at
them. Myra runs down to the basement where we keep the cedar
chest. She's looking for the dress she wore last year for Bonds for
Israel. She can't find the light, trips down the stairs, passes out in the
dark. I run downstairs looking for Myra, notice the basement door is
open, and afraid the strange-looking kid is coming back, I lock the
door, not knowing Myra is still down there. Then I run upstairs to

take some aspirin because my ear lobe is killing me from the hole in it. But the blood on my fingers gets in my eyes and by mistake I take four Valium instead. I hear the guests downstairs and I want to tell them to look for Myra. But suddenly, I can't talk from the Valium, and I'm bleeding on the white rug. So I start to write a note explaining what happened, but the note looks like gibberish. And I'm afraid they'll think it was a suicide note and they'll call the police and my friend Glenn Cooper was coming and it would be very bad for his campaign to get mixed up with a suicide, so I tore the note up and flushed it down the toilet, just as they walked into my room. They're yelling at me, "What happened? What happened?" And before I could tell them what happened, I passed out on the bed. And that's the whole goddamn story, as sure as my name is . . . (*He opens his robe to expose the monogram "CB" on the pajamas.*) . . . Charley Brock.

LOST in YONKERS

Premièred December 31, 1990
at the Center for the Performing Arts,
Winston-Salem, North Carolina

Directed by Gene Saks

CAST

Jay	Jamie Marsh
Arty	Danny Gerard
Eddie	Mark Blum
Bella	Mercedes Ruehl
Grandma Kurnitz	Irene Worth
Louie	Kevin Spacy
Gert	Lauren Klein

The action of the play takes place in an apartment above an ice cream-candy store in Yonkers.

Eddie Kurnitz, a deeply-in-debt widower, leaves his sons, Jay and Arty, with their grandmother until he can regain financial solvency. Grandmother Kurnitz is a disabled old-world matriarch who is looked after by her daughter Bella, a pretty woman of diminished mental capacity who also assists in managing the candy store below their apartment. Jay and Arty do their best to adapt in spite of their Grandmother's cold, unloving attitude, an attitude that has had negative psychological impact upon her children. The boys are buoyed only by the gentle kindness of Bella and letters from their father.

Bella, desperately needing to be touched and loved, finds vicarious release in movies and random forays with men. This leads to her meeting a kindred spirit in the person of John, a child-like usher at a local theater. She confides in Jay and Arty that they plan to marry, open a restaurant, and bear children. She asks for their support when she breaks the news to Grandma.

Into the mix comes younger son Louie, a street-wise man of specious character who is in hiding from persons outside the law. He is tough and cocky, the antithesis of brother Eddie, a hardened byproduct of his emotionally iron mother. Louie temporarily moves into the apartment, sharing the bedroom with Jay and Arty (who find him fascinating).

Hoping to gain support for her announcement of marriage, Bella invites sister Gert to dinner. (Gert, another casualty of steel-hearted Grandma, suffers from a psychologically induced respiratory problem.) When Bella makes her plans known, she is severely criticized by Louie and is coldly-rejected by Grandma, who leaves the dinner table and retreats to her room. Bella leaves home.

When Bella returns after staying with Gert for a few days, she confronts Grandma honestly, expressing her need for love, the love that her mother has withheld. During this cathartic exchange we are taken to the core of Grandma's austerity; she has always punished herself for the premature deaths of her children Aron and Rose, and feels that her surviving them is a sin for which she deserves punishment. Bella tells Grandma that there will be no wedding because John is not willing to leave his parents and the safe confines of the darkened theater. But she has changed and—even though child-like—will never go back to being an unloved victim.

After nine months, Eddie returns to pick up his sons, who have not only survived their ordeal, they have matured as a result of dealing with it. They have grown and so has Grandma, and we sense a relaxation of her rigidity as the boys make their farewells and Bella plans for her future as a real person.

Eddie. ACT I. Scene i.

Eddie has asked his mother for permission to leave sons Jay and Arty with her while he is working as a traveling salesman. Awaiting her decision, he explains to the boys the reasons for his actions.

EDDIE

We're not rich people, boys. I know that doesn't come as a surprise to you . . . But I'm going to tell you something now I hoped I'd never have to tell you in my life . . . The doctors, the hospital, cost me everything I had . . . I was broke and I went into debt . . . So I went to a man . . . A loan shark . . . A money-lender . . . I couldn't go to a bank because they don't let you put up heartbreak and pain as collateral . . . A loan shark doesn't need collateral . . . His collateral is your desparation . . . So he gives you his money . . . And he's got a clock . . . And what it keeps time of is your promise . . . If you keep your promise, he turns off the clock . . . and if not, it keeps ticking . . . and after a while, your heart starts ticking louder than his clock . . . Understand something. This man kept your mother alive . . . It was his painkillers that made her last days bearable . . . And for that I'm grateful . . . Jay! Remember what I taught you about taking things from people?

Intervening speech. Jay: (*Nods.*) Naver take because you'll always be obligated.

EDDIE (*cont'd.*)

So you never take for yourself . . . But for someone you love, there comes a time when you have no choice . . . There's a man in New York I owe . . . Nine thousand dollars . . . I could work and save four more years and I won't have nine thousand dollars . . . He wants his money this year. To his credit, I'll say one thing. He sent flowers to the funeral. No extra charge on my bill . . .

Intervening speech. Jay: Pop—

EDDIE (*cont'd.*)

Let me finish . . . There is no way I can pay this man back . . . So what'll he do? Kill me? . . . Maybe . . . If he kills me, he not only loses his money, it'll probably cost him again for the flowers for *my* funeral . . . I needed a miracle . . . And the miracle happened . . . This country went to war . . . A war between us and the Japanese and the Germans . . . And if my mother didn't come to this country thirty-five hears ago, I could have been fighting for the other side . . . Except I don't think they're putting guns in the hands of Jews over there . . . Let me tell you something. I love this country. Because they took in the Jews. They took in the Irish, the Italians and everyone else . . . Remember this. There's a lot of Germans in this country fighting for America, but there are no Americans over there fighting for Germany . . . I hate this war, and God forgive me for saying this, but it's going to save my life . . . There are jobs I can get now that I could never get before . . . And I got a job . . . I'm working for a company that sells scarp iron . . . I thought you threw scarp iron away. Now they're building ships with it . . . Without even the slightest idea of what I'm doing, I can make that nine thousand dollars in less than a year . . .

Intervening speech. Jay: That's great, Pop.

EDDIE (*cont'd.*)

Don't say it till I finish . . . The factories that I would sell are in the south . . . Georgia, Kentucky, Louisana, Texas, even New Mexico . . . I'd be gone about ten months . . . Living in trains, buses, hotels, any place I can find a room . . . We'd be free and clear and back together again in less than a year . . . Okay? So now comes the question, where do you two live while I'm gone?

Grandma. ACT I. Scene i.

Grandma coldly rejects Eddie's request to allow the boys to stay with her while he is working. Her words reveal the reasons for her stridency and her children's emotional frailties.

GRANDMA

So! You haff no place else to go. Dot's vy you vant to live vith Grandma . . . All right . . . So now Grandma vill tell you vy she doesn't tink you should live vit her . . . Dis house is no place for boys. I'm am an old woman. I don't like to talk. I don't like noise. I don't like people in my house. I had six children once, I don't need more again . . . Bella and I take care of the store six days a veek and on Sunday ve rest. Today is Sunday and I'm not resting . . . Bella is not—she's not goot vit people too long. A little bit yes, then she gets too excited . . . You understand vot I'm saying? . . . Vot vould you do here? There's no games in dis house. There's no toys in dis house. I don't like the radio after six o'clock. The news, yes, dot's all . . . Ve go to sleep nine o'clock, ve get up five o'clock. I don't have friends. Bella don't have friends. You vould not be happy here. And unhappy boys I don't need.

Intervening speech. Eddie: Momma, can I say something—?

GRANDMA *(cont'd.)*

(Holds up a cane.) No! I'll just say someting . . . I tink about dis inside. Because anger hass been in me for a long time . . . Vy should I do dis? . . . Vot do I owe your father? . . . Ven did he ever come

around here after he married your mother? I never saw him . . . Because she turned him against me. His own mother . . . She didn't like me, I didn't like her. I'm not afraid to tell da truth either . . . I don't vish anybody's death. Maybe she vas a goot mother to you, may she rest in peace, to me she vas nothing . . . And your father vas afraid of her. Dot's vy he stopped coming here. You're big boys now, how many times haff I seen you since you were born? Four, five times? . . . Dose are not grandchildren. Dose are strangers . . . And now he comes to me for help? . . . he cried in my bedroom. Not like a man, like a child he cried. He vas always dot vay . . . I buried a husband and two children und I didn't cry. I didn't haff time. Bella vas born vit scarlet fever and she didn't talk until she vas five years old, und I didn't cry . . . Your father's sister, Gertrude, can't talk vitout choking und I didn't cry. . . . Und maybe one day, they'll find Louie dead in da street und I von't cry . . . Dot's how I vas raised. To be strong. Ven dey beat us vit sticks in Germany ven ve vere children, I didn't cry . . . You don't survive in dis vorld vitout being like steel. Your father vants you to grow up, first let *him* grown up . . . Ven he learns to be a father, like I learned to be a mother, den he'll be a man. Den he von't need my help . . . You tink I'm cruel? You tink I'm a terrible person? Dot a grandmother should say tings like dis? I can see it in your faces vot you tink . . . Goot, it'll make you hard. It'll make you strong. Den you'll be able, to take care of yourselves vitout *any*body's help . . . So dot's my decision. Maybe one day you'll tank me for it. (*She gets up.*) Give da boys an ice cream cone, Bella. Den come inside and finish my legs.

Eddie. ACT I. Scene i.

This is Eddie's immediate response to Grandma's speech above, and in it is the crux of his, Bella's, Louie's, and Gertrude's problems— lack of parental compassion and love. At the conclusion of this

*monologue, Bella threatens Grandma with leaving if the boys are not
allowed to stay.*

EDDIE

(*Without anger.*) . . . You're right, Momma. I am the weak one. I am
the crybaby . . . Always was. When you wouldn't pick me up and
hug me as a child, I cried . . . When my brother and sister died, I
cried . . . And I still haven't stopped crying since Evelyn died . . . But
you're wrong about one thing. She never turned me against you. She
turned me towards *her* . . . To loving, to caring, to holding someone
when they needed holding . . . I'm sorry about not bringing the boys
out here more. Maybe the reason I didn't was because I was afraid
they'd learn something here that I tried to forget . . . Maybe they just
learned it today . . . I'm sorry I bothered you on your Sunday. I'm
sorry I imposed on your rest. I'm sorry about what they did to you as
a child in Berlin. I'm sure it was terrible. But this is Yonkers,
Momma. I'm not angry at you for turning me and the boys down. I'm
angry at myself for not knowing better . . . Take care of yourself,
Momma . . . Never mind the ice cream cones, Bella. I used up all my
obligations for this year. (*He crosses to the door.*) Come on, boys.
We're going.

Louie. ACT I. Scene iv.

*In this story about the theft of ice cream from the store below, Uncle
Louie tells Jay and Arty the difference between him and their father.
Here we can see how their extreme personality traits were formed by
their reaction to the hardness of their mother.*

LOUIE

Yeah, well, he was no good at it anyway. Ma knew what was goin'
on. She could tell if there was salt missin' from a pretzel . . . But she

wouldn't say nothin'. She'd come up from the store with milk, sid-down for breakfast, knowin' that two scoops of everything was missin', and she'd just stare at you . . . right into your eyeballs, pupil to pupil . . . never blinkin' . . . Her eyes looked like two District Attorneys . . . and Eddie couldn't take the pressure. He'd always crack. Tears would start rollin' down his checks like a wet confession . . . and whack, he'd get that big German right hand across the head . . . But not me . . . I'd stare her right back until her eyelids started to weigh ten pounds each . . . And she'd turn away from me, down for the count . . . And you know what? She loved it . . . because I knew how to take care of myself . . . Yeah, me and Ma loved to put on the gloves and go the distance.

Louie. Act II. Scene i.

Louie tells Jay and Arty how Grandma used to lock the children in the closet for hours for minor infractions. Her cruel forms of discipline had negative effects that have carried forward to the present, and they explain Gertrude's respiratory dysfunction.

Preceding speech. Arty: Did you ever want to run away?

LOUIE

I did. Twelve times. Still a record in Yonkers. The last time she wouldn't take me back. Tole the policeman she didn't know me. I had no place to go so I lived under the house with a couple of cats for two weeks. Dead of winter. Bella would come out and bring me sandwiches, a blanket, a couple of candles. Mom caught her and put her in the closet overnight. But Bella don't understand anything so she thought it was kinda fun. Or maybe she thought it was the safest place to be . . . Now, Gert—Gert was more scared than your old man. Gert used to talk in her sleep and Mom heard her one night sayin' things she didn't like. So Gert didn't get supper that week. Until she learned to sleep holdin' her breath.

Jay. ACT II. Scene i.

Arty has been curious about the contents of a black bag that Louie has brought with him. When Louie attempts to intimidate him into opening the bag, Jay steps forward and protects him, and also defends his father in a show of loyalty and courage.

JAY

Don't do it, Arty . . . Leave him alone, Uncle Louie. You want the bag open, do it yourself. (*He takes the bag from Arty and tosses it at Louie's feet.*) Maybe you don't rob banks or grocery stores or little old women. You're worse than that. You're a bully. You pick on a couple of kids. Your own nephews. You make fun of my father because he cried and was afraid of Grandma. Well, everyone in *Yonkers* is afraid of Grandma . . . And let me tell you something about my father. At least he's doing something in this war. He sick and he's tired but he's out there selling iron to make ships, and tanks and cannons, and I'm proud of him. What are *you* doing? Hiding in your mother's apartment and scaring little kids and acting like Humphrey Bogart . . . Well, you're no Humphrey Bogart . . . And I'll tell you something else—No. That's all.

Bella. ACT II. Scene ii.

When Bella discloses her plans to marry one of her own ilk, a child-like, forty-year-old usher, she is admonished by Louie, who cannot believe that the man would want her for herself. Hurt, desperately needing love, Bella exposes the family tragedy in her plea for her mother to sanction the union.

BELLA

You think I can't have healthy babies, Momma? Well, I can . . . I'm as strong as an ox. I've worked in that store and taken care of you by myself since I'm twelve years old, that's how strong I am . . . Like *steel*, Momma. Isn't that how we're supposed to be? . . . But my babies won't die because I'll love them and take care of them . . . And they won't get sick like me or Gert or be weak like Eddie and Louie . . . My babies will be happier than we were because I'll teach them to be happy . . . Not to grow up and run away or never visit when they're older and not be able to breathe because they're so frightened . . . and never, *ever* to make them spend their lives rubbing my back and legs because you never had anyone around who loved you enough to want to touch you because you made it so clear you never wanted to be touched with love . . . Do you know what it's like to touch steel, Momma? It's hard and it's cold and I want to be warm and soft with my children . . . Let me have my babies, Momma. Because I have to love somebody. I have to love someone who'll love me back before I die . . . Give me that, Momma, and I promise you, you'll never worry about being alone . . . Because you'll have us . . . Me and my husband and my babies . . . Louie, tell her how wonderful that would be . . . Gert, wouldn't that make her happy? . . . Momma? . . . Please say yes . . . I need you to say yes . . . Please?

Bella. ACT II. Scene iii.

Bella, rejected by her mother, has returned home after spending a few days with her sister Gertrude. In a scene between her and her mother, she explains that even though she possesses a child-like mind, she has the desires of a woman. In the following speech, she reveals sexual experiences that were motivated by a craving for intimacy and were substitutes for the love she never received at home.

BELLA

No! You *have* to listen, Momma . . . When I was in school, I let boys touch me . . . And boys that I met in the park . . . And in the movies . . . Even boys that I met here in the store . . . Nights when you were asleep, I went down and let them in . . . And just not boys, Momma . . . men too.

Intervening speech. Grandma: Stop dis, Bella. You don't know vot you're saying . . . You dream these things in your head.

BELLA (*cont'd.*)

I needed somebody to touch me, Momma. Somebody to hold me. To tell me I was pretty . . . *You* never told me that. Some even told me they loved me but I never believed them because I knew what they wanted from me . . . Except John. He *did* love me. Because he understood me. Because he was like me. He was the only one I ever felt safe with. And I thought maybe for the first time I *could* be happy . . . That's why I ran away. I even brought the five thousand dollars to give to him for the restaurant. Then maybe he'd find the courage to leave home too.

JAKE'S WOMEN

Premièred March 24, 1992 at the
Neil Simon Theatre, New York City

Directed by Gene Saks

CAST

Jake	Alan Alda
Maggie	Helen Shaver
Karen	Brenda Vaccaro
Molly (at 12)	Genia Michaela
Molly (at 21)	Tracy Pollan
Edith	Joyce Van Patten
Julie	Kate Burton
Sheila	Talia Balsam

The action of the play takes place in Jake's apartment in Soho and in his mind.

Jake, a writer, immerses himself in the world of fiction as a way of avoiding honest interaction and expressing real feelings. He is more comfortable facing his word processor than facing life's realties. When a marital crisis arises, he turns to the comfortable world of his creative imagination because it affords him a means of controlling events and outcomes. Through a mixture of flashbacks, fantasies and reality, we meet Jake's women: his first wife, who was tragically killed in an automobile accident; his daughter as both a juvenile and an adult; his abrasive analyst; his authoritative sister; his current wife, who is asking for a six-months separation; and a prospective third wife. Although a comedy, the play is a study of a person haunted by an inability to relinquish control, face truth, and come to terms with honest feelings.

Jake. ACT I.

After an imaginary interlude with his wife, Maggie, during which he recalls their first meeting, Jake prepares for her actual return and a confrontation regarding marital problems. Much more comfortable with products of his creative imagination, he has great trepidation about facing the actual Maggie and the real problems they share. This speech follows the imaginary Maggie's comment that Jake is scared stiff about what might occur later because he can't control real events. Near the conclusion of the monologue Jake asks for help from his sister Karen and is consoled by the fact that her advice will be supportive because he will be scripting the dialogue. More self-delusion.

JAKE

(*Speaking to the audience.*) She's right, you know. Reality is a bummer. God, how much better writing is. (*He points to his office.*) That little room up there is eight by ten feet but to me it's the world. The universe! You don't get to play God, you get to *be* God! . . . Push time backwards or forwards or put it on hold. Bend it, twist it, tie it in knots or tie it in ribbons, the choice is yours. And oh, what choices . . . The downside? You get to be a slave to the thing you love. Eight hours go by up there in ten minutes and that ten minutes is captured forever on paper . . . but the eight hours of your life is gone and you'll never see those again, brother . . . How much living have I missed these last thirty years? . . . And is creative pleasure better than real pleasure? . . . We're all writers in a sense, aren't we? . . . You're driving in your car to work, having an imaginary conversation with your wife. She says this, you say that, she says that, you say this. She's so damn stubborn and intractable—only she's not saying it. You wrote it! You're bright, witty and clever and she's a pain in the kind of victory is that? (*He looks at his watch.*) Maggie'll be home soon, knowing something is up with us and she'll be armed to the teeth with honesty. Honest can bring a writer to his knees and Maggie's got enough to bring me to my hips. (*He calls out.*) Karen! I need help. (*To the audience.*) My sister Karen is no wizard but she *is* family. Married, divorced, went to NYU film school. Made a three-hour student film of her, just sitting on a kitchen chair called, *Loneliness* . . . But she'll be on my side. Loving, encouraging, sympathetic, because that's how I need her and how I'll make her. And no matter what she's doing, she'll come the minute I think of her. (*He calls out.*) Karen! It's Jake.

Maggie. ACT I.

Maggie, due to a conventional Midwestern upbringing, has never really felt fulfilled. And her marriage to Jake hasn't contributed to her development as a fully realized, independent woman. She is tired of living in the shadow of Jake's deceased wife, Julie, and playing second fiddle to Jake's work. Her climb up the corporate ladder has put an even greater strain on her marriage because Jake is threatened by her independence and the fact that he cannot control her existence. Angry and unhappy, she has overcompensated by throwing herself into her corporate life—and into bed with a fellow employee while in Chicago on business. Feeling contrite, claustrophobic, and isolated, she has, over Jake's vehement objections, decided on a six-months' trial separation.

Jake's preceding speech: The first team? Jesus, you devoted so much of this marriage trying to become Chairman of the Board, I never saw you for half of those eight years. I don't know whose dream you were trying to fulfill, but it sure as hell wasn't mine.

MAGGIE

Well, unfortunately, it wasn't mine either. For as long as I can remember, I was molded and shaped in the form of somebody *else's* concept of a woman, never mine. The church taught it to me, parochial schools taught it to me, my mother, my father—God, you couldn't get out of the Midwest without its stamp of approval. I was taught to be a good girl, a wife and a mother but never a person. You could be a carbon copy but don't mess with being an original. That's what you married eight years ago, Jake. A good girl. As good and as obedient as my mother, never suspecting, of course, that it was three martinis a day that kept her obedient . . . And then one day I woke up and said to myself, "I don't want to be anyone's concept of me except me . . . not even Jake's" . . . You are so important to me, but you're also so consumed with creating your own images and characters, planning every detail in their life, molding them and shaping them into *your* creations, *your* concepts. And I said, "Jesus, I just left all this in Michigan, what do I want it in New York for?" . . . And the minute I tried to step out on my own, to try to be someone *I* created, that *I* controlled, you made me pay so dearly for it. You made me feel like a plagiarist . . . And so one day in Chicago, I let myself become a very bad little girl. The next morning I looked in the mirror and I sure didn't like what I saw. But I saw the possibility of becoming someone who would have to be accepted on *her* terms and certainly not someone who was considered a rewrite of someone else. And until you begin to see *me*, Jake, *my* Maggie, I am getting out of this house, out of this life and out of your word processor . . . I may be making the biggest mistake of my life but at least it'll be mine . . . Dear Lord, Creator of the Universe, forgive me. And if not, not.

Jake. ACT I.

Jake's imaginary conversation with his deceased wife, Julie, has just been interrupted by a phone call from their daughter Molly, a student at Amherst. Jake discerns from the tone of her voice that she is aware of the marital problems between Maggie and him. At the end of his speech, he summons a flashback scene of the first meeting between Maggie and Molly.

JAKE

(*Back into PHONE.*) Molly? Sorry . . . A little hectic today . . . Listen, hon. There's a little trouble here . . . No, no . . . domestic . . . Can we talk about it later? . . . Thanks . . . Maggie's upstairs . . . Listen, don't tell her I said anything . . . I love you too . . . Hold on. (*He presses another button, then into PHONE.*) Hi. It's Molly. Do you want to talk to her? . . . No, I just said there were problems but I didn't go into any details . . . I think so too . . . All right. Hold on. (*He switches buttons again, then hangs up. He looks up at the audience. To audience.*) Molly knew what was wrong without me even telling her. She knew me better than I knew myself . . . I have a theory that wisdom doesn't come with age. It comes at childhood, peaks around eighteen, then slides slowly down the scale into adulthood . . . Parents express anger at a child by saying, "You ungrateful little brat. You'll never amount to anything" . . . But kids are creative. They express anger by going to school and drawing a picture of you with the head of a gargoyle . . . God has protected children with a purity of spirit and the ability to see things as they really are. They have an uncanny knack for speaking simple truths . . . Molly, as young as she is, had the one quality I was never able to find, or worse still, never able to accept in another human being . . . Trust! (*He crosses.*) For example, on the first day that she and Maggie met eight years ago, as certain as I was about Maggie, it was Molly alone

whose stamp of approval I needed. I remember it as if it were yesterday. (*He snaps his fingers . . . MAGGIE comes on. This is MAGGIE
eight years ago.*)

Karen. ACT II.

*During the six months since Maggie left him, Jake's life has been a
lonely, miserable mess. His creative juices have run dry, his forays
into dating have been totally unfulfilling experiences, and he cannot
stop his imagination from calling up unwanted visitations, like this
one from his sister Karen, during which she admonishes him for his
inability to open up, relinquish control, and experience honest feelings.*

KAREN

I said, "Aha, *that* you're afraid of." I think you're afraid to lose control in a relationship with a woman. To let a woman in so close, so
deep inside of you, that she'll gobble you up and you'll lose
whatever you think you are. You always have to be the Master, Jake.
The Master, the Conductor, the Director and the Attorney General.
You don't think it's strange that you sit around here thinking about
women and making up what they say to you? And then you think up
that *we* make up that we come over here on our own? Come on! How
much more control do you want? . . . They love you, they leave you,
they come back to you, they worry about you, the die, they live, They
grow up, they fall down, they fight for you, they cry for you—it's a
three-ring circus in here and all the horses and lions and elephants
are women . . . You're the star of the show, Jake. You're the one they
shoot out of a cannon and you fly around the tent with an American
flag in your mouth and all the women go crazy and faint and they
take them away to hospitals . . . the trouble is—it's very hard to get

close to a man who's flying around in a tent with a flag in his mouth. That's what I call trouble with intimacy.

Jake. ACT II.

Jake can no longer control the products of his imagination. After a disruptive, imagined scene with his sister Karen and his shrink, Edith, he is fearful for his sanity—which he expresses in this mono-logue. The speech is interrupted by an actual visit from his current girlfriend, Sheila, an interruption he welcomes as a means of con-necting with a person of corporeal nature.

JAKE

(*Turns to the audience.*) You want to know how low I've sunk? (*He points to the PHONE.*) I never spoke to Edith. I called my service. I actually made a phone call pretending I was speaking to the *real* Edith to scare the Edith and Karen in my head out of here . . . I tricked myself and I fell for it . . . The thing about going crazy is that it makes you incredibly smart, in a stupid sort of way. (*He starts to move down.*) But I do feel like I'm losing a grip on myself. As if I'm spiraling down in diminishing circles like water being drained from a bathtub, and suddenly, my big toe is being sucked down into the hole and I'm screaming for my life . . . No. Not my life. My mother . . . Why, tell me why, it's always your mother? It's never your father or your uncle or a second cousin from Detroit . . . I was five years old in a third-floor apartment in the Bronx, waking up from a nap and there's no one there. My mother is on the *fourth* floor visiting a neighbor. I'm terrified. Why doesn't she hear me? Why doesn't she come? And by the time she comes, it's too late. Your basic Freudian mother abandonment trauma has set in like cement . . . I never trusted her again. (*The INTERCOM BUZZES.*) What was that? . . . Oh, the buzzer . . . God, I'm a bundle of nerves . . . (*He picks it up.*)

Yes? . . . Oh, Sheila? . . . What a suprise, Sheila . . . Where are you, Sheila? . . . Oh, of course. Downstairs . . . sure. Come on up, Sheila. (*To audience.*) But Jake is doomed? Not by a long shot. There's Sheila. Another woman to the rescue . . . Another woman . . . It's always another woman . . . Stop it, Jake . . . You can handle it, Jake. Get a hold of yourself, Jake . . . Get a grip on yourself . . .

Jake. ACT II.

In order to get rid of girlfriend Sheila, Jake contrives an imagined scene between Sheila, Maggie, and himself. His off-the-wall behavior scares Sheila off and out of his life, and once again relieves him from facing an unpleasant situation—coming to grips with the truth. In the aftermath of this scene, the imagined Maggie rightly accuses him of avoiding honest confrontation and, pointing upstairs to where he does his creative writing, declares, " . . . leave your work up there where it belongs. That's writing—this is living. . . ." After she exits his memory, Jake delivers the following monologue about one of the formative childhood experiences that ruptured his ability to trust. At the end of this speech, Julie, his long-dead wife, springs from his imagination.

JAKE

(*Turns to the audience.*) I have the feeling I'm trying to put together a jigsaw puzzle that has no picture on it . . . I'm a blank, waiting to fill in who I am . . . How did I get to be this way? . . . That's not a rhetorical question. I mean, if you know, please tell me . . . Okay, Jake. Go back to the beginning. That's what Edith always says . . . Here's another Mother story . . . I'm six years old, sitting in the kitchen with my mother, watching her shell peas . . . And on the floor I see a roach . . . My Mother, faster than a speeding train, takes a newspaper and splats it against the baseboard . . . "Where do roaches come from?" I ask my mother . . . "From the dirt," she answers . . . "You mean," I say, "the roaches like to live in the dirt and eat it?" . . . "No," says Mom. "The dirt turns *into* roaches." And I go back into my room, lay on the bed and say to myself, "The dirt turns into roaches" . . . And the realization hits me . . . My mother is dumb . . . And I know instinctively that six years old is too soon to find out that your mother is dumb . . . Because I'm banking my whole childhood on this woman taking care of me . . . And so I decided on that day, I would never depend on anyone except myself . . . I loved my mother, but I never asked her any more questions . . . The trouble is, here I am today at the age of fifty-three, without any answers . . . Oh my God, Julie!

Jake. Act II.

After six months of separation, Maggie drops by to see Jake. Initially there is stilted small-talk until Maggie informs Jake that she is having dinner with a man who is going to propose marriage. Then the conversation turns serious. Maggie misses Jake and still cares for him, but she tells him that even though they are just inches away from reconciliation, their future is dim unless he can learn to trust his real feelings and stop living in a world of fiction were he is a manipulator, a voyeur hiding behind his characters. This interchange between them proves to be one of the most positive they've ever had, and we sense that Jake is nearing an epiphany. In the following speech, Jake recalls another childhood event that has had lasting negative effects. This cathartic revelation leads to Jake purging himself of the need to call up characters from his imagination, a breakthrough that is both stimulating and frightening.

JAKE

(*To the audience.*) Men have climbed mountains for women and crossed burning deserts for them, and I can't get to this one because I'm two lousy inches away . . . Maybe if I could put a little weight on around the midsection, I could squeeze across the finish line . . . Okay, so I need a catharsis, a bolt of lightning and a miracle . . . Where the hell do I shop for that? . . . Wait! Hold it! . . . One last Mother story . . . Make that a Mother and Father story . . . I feel a connection here . . . I am ten years old, walking down the street with my friend, Sal . . . And coming in the opposite direction is my father with a woman half his age . . . A chippie, they called them then . . . He doesn't see me but Sal says to me, "Hey, Jake. There's you father" . . . And I say to protect my father or my shame, "No, it's not. It just *looks* like my father." . . . What prompts me later that day to tell my mother about it is still unclear to me. I want to make things right but right for who? . . . When my father comes home later that night, my mother pulls him into my bedroom, turns on the lights and screams at me, "Tell him, Jake. Tell him what you told me you saw today." . . . I want to run as fast as I can or die on the spot, but my mother won't be denied. I tell my father what I saw . . . And he looks me in the eye and says, "You're a liar. You saw someone else, not me" . . . He makes me pay for his indiscretion . . . I hate my father for betraying my mother, hate my mother for betraying me and hate myself for betraying them both . . . It did, in time, pass and maybe was even forgotten in the forty years that eventually buried them both . . . But I can't help feeling that three betrayals in one day could eventually make two inches to cross—a very long trip for someone who never learned to trust again . . . So what would that be? A small catharsis? (*Looks off.*) What do you think, Karen? . . . Karen? . . . Where are you? . . . Karen, I'm calling you. (*To audience.*) She's never done this before . . . Karen, it's Jake. I need you . . . Come on, wear anything you want, I'll pay for it. Where are you? (*To audi-*

ence.) This is scary. Don't go away. I don't feel like being alone right now . . . Edith! . . . Please come out. I can't wait till our appointment on Tuesday . . . I need a quick fix. A couple of laughs . . . I need the jokes, the kidding around. *Love Yourself, Fuck Them*, that was funny, wasn't it? . . . Molly? Julie? Not even you? . . . You want to see each other again, I'll set it up. I'll order in pizzas, you can spend the whole day gabbing and gorging yourselves, whaddya say? (*To the audience*.) Jesus! I've been praying to get rid of them, *begging* for them to be gone and now that they're not here I feel empty. I feel scared, I feel stark naked . . . Jesus, this is hard. My goddamn heart is palpitating . . . I can hardly breathe . . .what is this? . . . Is this going crazy? Is this going mad? . . . Or is this the miracle? . . . I mean she already got her catharsis, maybe this is the freaking miracle . . . (*Looks around*.) So what have we got left? A bolt of lightning . . . (*He moves away*.) Better get away from anything metal . . . Rubber? Where's rubber? . . . (*He walks around. We suddenly hear a VOICE, a VOICE not clear as to gender or age*.)

Jake. ACT II.

Jake is startled and confused by the intrusion of a disembodied voice, a "voice" that says, "I love you . . . and I forgive you." He mistakenly assumes that it is his mother, but awakens to the fact that is his voice forgiving her. *In this climax speech, Jake realizes that forgiveness is a stepping stone to self-realization. At the conclusion of the monologue, the women of Jake's imagination appear for a final farewell. He no longer needs them. He needs Maggie, the real and tangible Maggie, and he expresses this with a shout, "Maggie! I want Maggie!" The doorbell sounds. It is Maggie. She has canceled her engagement in favor of returning to Jake and working things out between them. At this, the imaginary Julie states, "Let's go,*

Ladies . . . I don't think we live here any more." One by one, they *quickly disappear.*

JAKE

What have you got, your own sound system? . . . What are you doing this for, Mom? . . . If you forgive me, what is it you forgive me for? (*To the audience.*) Am I really hearing her or is this my imagination? . . . No, this is coming from someplace else . . . Some deep place I've never tapped into before. Only what's the point of it? (*To Voice.*) What are you doing this for, Ma?

Intervening speech. Voice: (*From another speaker.*) Think about it, Jake. You'll figure it out.

JAKE (*cont'd.*)

(*Speaks to the audience.*) Thank God Sheila isn't here, her hair would turn white by now . . . "Think about it, Jake. You'll figure it out." . . . My mother was never articulate before and suddenly she gives me the hieroglyphics to work out . . . "Think about it, you'll figure it out." . . . No, as I said, I loved my mother, but I didn't trust her before and I don't trust her now. (*He starts up the steps, stops, then comes back down.*) . . . Wait a minute, wait a minute, hold it . . . That's not my mother's voice. It didn't sound like her . . . It sounded like—like me . . . Jesus! It was *my* voice. I had it all turned around . . . It was me saying to my mother, "I love you, Mom . . . and I forgive you" . . . (*He stops, catches himself, then moves Downstage.*) I love you, Mom . . . and I forgive you. (*He takes a second, then looks at audience.*) I think you have to forgive those you love before you can forgive yourself . . . And so Maggie got her bolt of lightning. (*He starts up to his office.*) So what do I do now? Call the restaurant and say to the maitre d', "Please tell the pretty lady in the beige suit her husband called and said, 'Just had the big three, hurry home'"? . . . (*He sits at his desk.*) No. Nothing in life gets resolved that fast. (*He turns, looks at the typewriter, when suddenly we hear music from downstairs. To audience.*) Did I leave the stereo on? . . . Or are my imaginary conversations turning into musicals now?

(*OLDER MOLLY, EDITH, KAREN, JULIE, SHEILA and YOUNGER MOLLY all appear suddenly from doors, from the balconies on both sides, all in party dresses.*)

ABOUT NEIL SIMON

Neil Simon was born in New York City, New York, in 1927 and graduated from New York University. He holds an Honorary Doctorate of Humane Letters from Hofstra University and an Honorary Doctorate from Williams College. His plays are *Come Blow Your Horn, Little Me* (musical), *Barefoot in the Park, The Odd Couple, Sweet Charity* (musical) *The Star-Spangled Girl, Plaza Suite, Promises, Promises* (musical), *Last of the Red Hot Lovers, The Gingerbread Lady, The Prisoner of Second Avenue, The Sunshine Boys, The Good Doctor, God's Favorite, California Suite, Chapter Two, They're Playing Our Song, I Ought to Be in Pictures, Fools, Little Me, Brighton Beach Memoirs, Biloxi Blues, The Odd Couple* (female version), *Broadway Bound, Rumors, Lost in Yonkers, Jake's Women, The Goodbye Girl (musical), Laughter on the 23rd Floor,* and *London Suite.*

Neil Simon has also written extensively for televsion and motion pictures. His awards include the Pulitzer Prize for *Lost in Yonkers*; Emmy awards for the "Sid Caesar Show" and "The Phil Silvers Show"; Tony awards for *The Odd Couple, Biloxi Blues* (Best Play), and *Lost in Yonkers* (Best Play); Tony nominations for *Little Me, Barefoot in the Park, Plaza Suite, Last of the Red Hot Lovers, The Prisoner of Second Avenue, Brighton Beach Memoirs, Broadway Bound,* and *Promises, Promises.* Mr. Simon also holds the Writers Guild screen award for *The Odd Couple* and *The Out-of-Towners*, the Writers Guild Laurel Award, the Evening Standard Award, the Sam S. Shubert award, and the American Comedy Award for Lifetime Achievement. He received the Writers Guild Screen Award nominations for *Barefoot in the Park* and an Oscar nomination for *The Odd Couple.*